The Black Subaltern

In *The Black Subaltern*, Shauna Knox revolts against the construct of the decontextualized self, electing instead to foreground the complex and problematic lived experience of the Black subaltern. Knox offers an account in which Black humanity is flattened, desubstantialized, and lost in a state of perpetual in-betweenness, which she coins subjective transmigration.

Over the course of this book, Knox weaves autobiographical vignettes featuring her own journey as a Jamaican migrant to the United States together with theoretical reflection in order to elaborate on the conditions of Black subalternity. She considers the dissolution and disappearance of the subaltern authentic self to be a prerequisite for acquiring access to society. Knox reflects that Black migrants, though rooted in a new country, still remain integrally engaged with their country of origin, and as such, ultimately find themselves in a purgatory of in-betweenness, inhabiting nowhere in particular.

This book's innovative use of postformal autobiography to give voice to the Black subaltern provides students and researchers across the humanities, Black studies, diaspora studies, anthropology, sociology, geopolitics, development, and philosophy with rich material for reflection and discussion.

Shauna Knox completed her doctoral studies at The George Washington University in 2019. She is a scholar activist with designated investment in exploring the elaborate subtleties of humanity at the nexus of Blackness, Womanism, and the Global South.

Routledge Studies on African and Black Diaspora

Series editors: Fassil Demissie, DePaul University and
Sandra Jackson, DePaul University

The Black Subaltern

An Intimate Witnessing

Shauna Knox

Routledge
Taylor & Francis Group

LONDON AND NEW YORK

First published 2022
by Routledge
4 Park Square, Milton Park, Abingdon, Oxon OX14 4RN

and by Routledge
605 Third Avenue, New York, NY 10158

Routledge is an imprint of the Taylor & Francis Group, an informa business

© 2022 Shauna Knox

The right of Shauna Knox to be identified as author of this work has been asserted in accordance with sections 77 and 78 of the Copyright, Designs and Patents Act 1988.

British Library Cataloguing-in-Publication Data
A catalogue record for this book is available from the British Library

Library of Congress Cataloging-in-Publication Data
Names: Knox, Shauna, author.
Title: The Black subaltern : an intimate witnessing / Shauna Knox.
Description: Abingdon, Oxon ; New York, NY : Routledge, 2022. |
Series: Routledge studies on African and Black diaspora |
Includes bibliographical references and index.
Identifiers: LCCN 2021061278 (print) | LCCN 2021061279 (ebook) |
ISBN 9781032128603 (hbk) | ISBN 9781032129105 (pbk) |
ISBN 9781003226802 (ebk)
Subjects: LCSH: Knox, Shauna. | Women immigrants–
United States–Biography. | Women, Black–United States–Biography. |
Jamaicans–United States–Biography. | African diaspora. |
Blacks–Race identity. | Marginality, Social–United States. |
United States–Race relations.
Classification: LCC HQ1120.U5 K66 2022 (print) |
LCC HQ1120.U5 (ebook) | DDC 305.800973–dc23/eng/20220211
LC record available at https://lccn.loc.gov/2021061278
LC ebook record available at https://lccn.loc.gov/2021061279

ISBN: 978-1-032-12860-3 (hbk)
ISBN: 978-1-032-12910-5 (pbk)
ISBN: 978-1-003-22680-2 (ebk)

DOI: 10.4324/9781003226802

Typeset in Times New Roman
by Newgen Publishing UK

Contents

Foreword
The Black Subaltern Writes Herself Into Visibility

Skillfully deploying autoethnography, *The Black Subaltern* audaciously traverses the treacherous geographical and ideological terrain that the self-reflexive narrator must negotiate in order to define her own identity and her contested place between worlds. Born in the United States to Jamaican parents, Shauna Knox foregrounds her enforced reduction to the liminal state of "anonymous, invisible Afro Caribbean American" in an alienating society that fails to acknowledge the complex ways in which identity is constructed for many hyphenated citizens.

Persuasively blending autoethnography and more "conventional" scholarship, Knox rewrites the dominant narrative of erasure and gives voice to silenced subjects, particularly migrants, who are often discounted in simplistic accounts of who constitutes the American nation. She deconstructs the native/foreign binary that is designed to limit identity to a single originary place. Knox cites anthropologists Nina Glick Schiller, Linda Basch, and Cristina Szanton Blanc who define the "transmigrant" as one who is grounded in the adoptive country but, nevertheless, remains rooted in the original home.

Transmigrancy is the central preoccupation of *The Black Subaltern*. Knox recounts her struggle to claim both Jamaica and the United States as home even though she is alienated from her truest self in both countries. Disdaining the label of subaltern, Knox nevertheless concedes its purchase in Western scholarship as a signifier of the alterity of those banished from the category of human: "The word subaltern emerges from postcolonial studies, to signify a colonial population that is systemically excluded from true social, political, and geopolitical power."

Knox summons a wide array of theorists across the disciplines in order to interrogate the processes of marginalization that relentlessly attempt to diminish the Black woman. Literary critic Carole Boyce Davies provides a foundational concept that recurs in *The Black Subaltern*: "flattened identity." Sociologist Cecilia Green theorizes the debilitating conflict between "respectability" and "self-respect" in delineating the positionality of Afro-Caribbean woman. Rebekah Kebede highlights skin bleaching as a pathological denial of blackness.

Psychiatrists Frederick Hickling and Gerard Hutchinson deploy the popular trope of the "roast breadfruit" to illuminate the psychosis of colonized subjects who are black on the outside and white inside. They manifest the "mimicry" which critical theorist Homi Bhabha highlights, following psychiatrist Frantz Fanon. Similarly, political philosopher Lloyd Best conceives the "Afro Saxon" as the colonized black subject masquerading as white.

Knox discloses an unsettling truth in *The Black Subaltern*: "When I wrote my first book about psychic colonization, and the publisher revised the title to remove the words 'Black,' 'Woman,' and 'Third World,' I was aware I would do something even before I decided." That first book, *Engaging Currere Toward Decolonization: Negotiating Black Womanhood through Autobiographical Analysis* confirms that Knox did, indeed, do something. She refused to delete "Black" and "Woman" from the title. "Third World" was erased but it remains as an absent presence.

The Black Subaltern is something else that Knox decided to do. Transmuting the essence of her academic book into a popular manifesto, Shauna Knox has brilliantly written herself out of anonymous invisibility and has carefully crafted her own authoritative narrative of transmigrant belonging. The harrowing journey to humanity that the Black, female subaltern must undertake is, ultimately, a rite of passage to a vibrant identity that women like Shauna Knox can unequivocally affirm.

Carolyn Cooper, Professor Emerita, The University of
the West Indies, Mona, Jamaica

Foreword

We all live, laugh, love, hate, cry, hurt, and die in a systematically anti-black world. And yet, as I have noted elsewhere, we do not all feel the idiosyncrasies of this reality in quite the same way. Though we have, as of late, endured an onslaught of hideous public displays of anti-Blackness manifested in state sanctioned killings of Black people, outlawing of Black history and Black hair, and an absurd number of Karen-antics, beneath it all is the always simmering everydayness of anti-Black images, sentiments, entrapments, enclosures, interactions, and relentless reinforcement by way of tedious kinds of physical, psychological, and spiritual violence. For the non-Black this may mean a disregard for or incomprehensibility of the person next door, or a co-worker, a student, or maybe even a close friend. But for the Black person it means wrestling everyday with a persistent, complex, and learned aversion to ourselves. For at least some part of our lives, if not all of our lives, we may go unaware of the depth and danger of the white thing within us, eating us from the inside out. We are devoured and disciplined by way of the Western curriculum of Blackness propagated in school, through the media, and sometimes just handed down from one trapped family member to another or in daily interactions with people still unable to register blackness, Black people as autonomous humans being. What does this feel like? What does it look like? Is there a language to capture the un/making of ourselves? Is there a way out?

In reading *The Black Subaltern* I was reassured that the only way "out" is in, into the contours of our innermost selves in an attempt to excavate the white thing within us. More than a theoretical meditation on the context and content of the Black subaltern, this work is a beautiful, painstaking, unsettling, and absolutely necessary rendering of the intimacies of anti-Blackness and how they manifest in implicit reproductions of the self. Through detailed re-memories, thoughtful reflection, and lingering questions, Shauna takes us into the classrooms, homeplaces, and seemingly mundane moments that map the un/making of herself as Black woman/child moving between homelands, languages, and histories. She draws on the concepts of flattening, disappearing, and transmigration in her efforts to speak what she has always felt but is only coming to know for sure through this powerful reckoning with the conditions of her feeling/knowing/being as a Black subaltern living/dying in a systematically anti-Black world.

I am taken with the text, because it's a reminder of a fact that seems to regularly slip loose in our efforts to make a better world. The systems, institutions, and structures that produce and reproduce the conditions of our oppression and subhumanity are not amorphous, abstract creations from on high and utterly out of our control, they are manmade, mostly mundane, and require the complicity of all of us at some level. To this end, the process of decolonizing calls on us to reach beyond protest and into the self and its collective as the most critical site of transformative possibility. *The Black Subaltern* is written in such a way that it doesn't just tell you what is happening, Shauna invites us into her most intimate thoughts and in a way that compels the reader to consider their own conditions of captivity, complicity, and (im)possibility.

Denise Taliaferro Baszile, Associate Dean and
Associate Professor, Miami University

Introduction

The Lord is near to all who call on him,
to all who call on him in truth.

Psalm 145:18

By design, this book resists the implications of the Eurocentric construct of the decontextualized self. In fact, this work bears witness to every imprint of context—both real and imagined—that offers the whole truth. The Black subaltern truth, whose testimony designates neither victim nor victor, will break every unspoken agreement; it will not be hidden in these words.

Let me tell you. There's a barrier that I was born into, there's a barrier that every small islander inherits, especially after colonialism, it is the barrier of self-contempt. You're a little place, you're not metropolitan, you wouldn't send men to the moon, you wouldn't invent the latest greatest computer, and you're not making any destructive weapons so you can kill the next man and take all his property and call it yours. You're a little island, so you're born into a situation where you feel lesser than other people, and it's called self-contempt. But once I began to shed my self-contempt after the power of this thing we call **mas** was revealed to me, it becomes a mission of mine to help people shed this self-contempt, because some people still don't understand that the things we do best are worthy of hallelujahs.

I start with the words that aren't mine, but those are the words of the iconic Guyanese–Trinidadian mas-man Peter Minshall, a god to many. Minshall is undoubtedly one of the Caribbean's greatest creatives, for his carnival work yes, but more for his art direction. This quote is from an interview that he did in 1995, just under one year after I became Minister of Culture, one year after I entered into the cabinet of Barbados.

DOI: 10.4324/9781003226802-1

This came after he had already directed, by the way, the opening ceremonies of the 1992 Barcelona Olympics, and the 1994 FIFA World Cup. He would go on to create the opening ceremonies for the 1996 Atlanta Olympics, the 2002 Salt Lake Winter Olympics, and the 2007 Cricket World Cup, which I had the honor to work with him personally on. Peter Minshall personifies world class—he is in the business, my friends, of the moonshots of which I spoke. While Minshall's artistic license frees him up to use terms such as self-contempt, to describe the Caribbean's underdevelopment, my technical sensibilities draw me to the more balanced phrasing of cultural confidence, or more to the point of lack of cultural confidence.

From political unrest, to gun violence, to bleaching of skin, the root of so many of our current regional problems boils down, I believe, to issues of identity and lack of cultural confidence. That is why in our own covenant of hope we literally put as the first chapter, identity and confidence, because without that we will go nowhere. That's why on my phone, I carry the picture of the late great Robert Nesta Marley, to remind me of two phrases: "Emancipate yourself from mental slavery" and of course "What does it profit a man to gain the world and to lose his soul?" Neither of those statements were original to Bob, but Bob understood the power of amplification with respect to them. He understood what it would do to our identity and to our cultural confidence. He understood that he was speaking each day, and every day, to that little girl and that little boy going into primary school, going into secondary school. At the end of the day, I ask this: Who are we? What makes us? How do we solve our own problems? What is our purpose? What is the value of our contribution?

As a region, we had all of this and so much more to consider, and then boops! comes COVID. But you will forgive me, as an eternal optimist, and an unwavering believer in the capacity of Caribbean people—I do not see identity issues as irreversible character flaws, nor do I see COVID-19 as an insurmountable challenge, nor do I believe that cultural values and cultural mores don't change. Fifty years ago we didn't play banja on a Sunday. What is banja you ask, any kind of music that is not hymns or gospel. But now throughout the region, that has changed. Some will argue, changed for the worse, some will argue changed for more tolerance, but whatever it is, the point is cultural values and cultural mores change. So rather I see this simply as part of a process of our development. I see it as part of our growing up, as part of the recognition that as adults we make choices and there are consequences to choices, and to that extent, our family, our parents, our extended family, and our community must help nurture us in the choices we have to make. We have moved my friends, beyond our tenuous toddler and moody teen years, where we were dependent on others for basic needs.

Beyond the rebelliousness of young adulthood, and the stabilizing middle-aged period, and now, like many 40- to 60-year-olds, we in the Caribbean are in a period of resilience and smart investment to secure our future. For countries, just like with humans, this natural cycle of development—of maturing and overcoming difficult periods—cannot be successfully achieved without first addressing some hard truths. As I say to my people in Barbados all the time, **yuh cyaa expeck to be an adult without having difficult conversations**—that's just life.

—Prime Minister of Barbados, Mia Mottley
(Granada Broadcasting Network, 2021)

This book is a difficult conversation. In it I explore the convoluted labyrinth of the libidinal economy of desire that demands the indiscriminate consumption of the Black subaltern—mind, body, and soul. It is in fact a conversation about life, about our lives. It is a conversation about the lived experiences of the Black subaltern woman, who is fragmented and subjectively scattered across the Atlantic in between "worlds," in her leaving and returning to the Global South.

The monograph presents an invitation into an intimate witnessing of what Jamaican Sociologist Orlando Patterson (2018) calls the social death of self-knowledge within the Black body. It exposes both the compromised imagined subjective renderings of what is, and the mirrored social agreements that settle into the stitching of what becomes conventional truth. This monograph disciplines its reader to remain tethered to the problematic malformations that emerge as a result of the subjective flattening, disappearance, and subjective transmigration of the Black subaltern. It presents no exemplar, and abandons the impulse to position the subject as virtuous victim, in search, instead, of an unmistakable humanity. Without counterfeit dichotomy or an editorialized interiority, the work is a treatise in surveilling the narrowed subject, in the precarious investigation of the situating of self, and the world around us. The book avoids the symbolic casting of paragons and their respective malefactors, and instead etches out a new space for subjective voice in conflict, within and without. It unveils thunderous theoretical elaborations in three parts, each labeled for their evocative unpacking of three select subjective phenomena endemic to Black subaltern life: Flattening, Disappearing, and Subjective Transmigration.

The word subaltern emerges from postcolonial studies to signify a colonial population that is systemically excluded from true social, political, and geopolitical power. The reach of the imperial control over the subaltern causes them to agree to this situating, without recognizing nor questioning the hegemonic arrangement. The introduction of each of the three theories—Flattening, Disappearing, and Subjective Transmigration—is followed by a series of vignettes that substantialize and enflesh each submission, they are not, however, to be read as distilled or reduced to essentialize the full breadth of each theory. In abandoning paradigmatic tropes and other moral imperatives that compel a simpler explanation, join me onward toward multiple dimensions of theoretical exploration in Black subalternity.

Reference

Granada Broadcasting Network. (2021, September 4). *Prime Minister of Barbados, Mia Mottley* [Status update]. Facebook. www.facebook.com/watch/?extid=WA-UNK-UNK-UNK-AN_GK0T-GK1C&v=614027803 101543

1 Flattening

In this section of the book, through postformal autobiography, I explore the phenomenon of the psychosocial flattening of the Black subaltern subject. In her text, *Black women, writing and identity: Migrations of the subject*, Carole Boyce-Davies (2002) proposes the concept of a 'flattened identity,' drawing on a Saudi woman's interview during the Gulf War in which she said "I resent not being able to drive an automobile more than I resent having to wear a veil." Boyce-Davies points to the woman's U.S. press-facing clarification of what truly inhibits her liberation, calling every witness beyond their imagined rendering of her domination into the fundamental truths of its reality. In the slippage that caused this exposure, Boyce-Davies investigates the "multiple significations of self-presentation and self-effacement," "double-voicedness," and the "motion between identities" as conscripts of "flattened identity." I extend Boyce-Davies's theorization of "flattened identity" beyond its re-negotiation between the subject and the other, in order to surveil the alterity that exists between the subject and the self. I analyze the internal reality of being flattened, scrutinizing the distortions and reductions of the subject that cause the self to lose dimension, deflate, and become pressed out. Beyond its defined designation as flattened identity, I investigate flatten[ing] as a condition of the colonized self, contemplating the implications of becoming a "spectator" to oneself, "crushed into a nonessential state" (Fanon, 2007).

In attempting this, I present 15 autobiographical vignettes, each of which features the multilayered experience of becoming flattened out elaborations which issue from the subjective locus. I attend deliberately to the intangible afflictions that issue from the flattening process, survey what metabolizes from it, and give voice to where it leaves the subaltern self. The accounts meticulously consider how the flattened Black subaltern subjectivity turns inward and regards itself, how it conceives of its own humanity, how it mediates the world's projections of its

DOI: 10.4324/9781003226802-2

sub-humanity, how it hardens, narrows, loses sight of self, endures the embezzlement of its access to its own empathy, and ultimately visits its infirmity on other Black subaltern beings. In order to reinflate that which has been flattened out within the subaltern subjectivity, I engage a politics of radical truth-telling and exposure, to release the hold of secrets Black subalterns are forced to keep and perform. In search of resuscitation, I chronicle the marvel of vacating the self, disclosing the terms of ugly bargains that only afford temporary stays of humanity, and offer visibility to the psychic devastation of subjective flattening as daily ritual.

I elucidate the poverty of thought and limitation on spirit that issues from an obligation to incessantly subvert the violent ignorance of Eurocentrism. I challenge the subjective instinct toward safekeeping, prodding at the morally reprehensible norms to which we have agreed if only to avoid the alternative, while attesting to the gradual yet demonstrable decay of self-betrayal. In a very practical sense, the Black subaltern must go numb and fixate on survival in order to stay alive. I illustrate the internal matrix of losing humanity as the subaltern subjectivity becomes remote from its selfhood. In these accounts of flattening, I read aloud the inscriptions of Blackness in their battle for significance within the imperialized body—conquered into respectability and an ethos of decorum that demands a deafening silence. I walk through the dynamics of the subaltern subjectivity, understanding itself as beast of burden, suffering the intrusion of Eurodominant civilizing impulses that prevent it from accessing authenticity for fear of complicit vulgarity. The translations of those interactions, intent on taming the subject out of its own validation, often meet proximate protest in the deep cultivation of internalized White supremacy, so that in a real sense, the Black subaltern is never really there. I address the castes of subalternity as deepened through the darkness of skin, the pursuit of passing into Whiteness and its privileges, and in-fighting between the hues. I discuss the true governance over Black subaltern bodies with flattened subjectivities, the implications of them existing for pleasure and curiosity in the world, and their fugitivity for refusing to die. In the naming of the unnamed and saying of the unsaid, this cannon breathes out new possibilities for subjective freedom for every flattened Black subaltern reader.

Falling Locs

My mother has always had long hair. When I was a child, a family picture loomed largely in our living room. Other pictures adorned the walls, but there was no question about which image commanded the space—that one textured, 20-by-24-inch canvas, set in a wooden frame, layered over by a yellow gold veneer made to look like it was put together in France in the eighteenth century. Our faces loomed so largely that they looked like alternate versions of us—I could never be fully sure they weren't watching me. Even with the lights on, I'd avert my gaze to be respectful just in case, but the one feature I couldn't pull myself away from was the luxurious bounty of my mother's hair. Bone straight, jet black, and flawlessly magnificent, it went past the draping of her white crêpe-de-chines shoulder pads with no evidence of ending. It was a thick velvet that controlled me, and I was desperate for my crinkly, stubborn plaits that were always standing in full salute, to fall like my mother's hair. I would stare at that picture for what felt like hours, willing my hair to go the way of my mother's, and lay gracefully to the small of my back. But it didn't. Instead, I spent every Saturday in the hair parlor, watching my hair disappoint me no matter what I tried to make it do.

When I turned 16, my dreams of glossy, supple hair left without warning. I cut all of my hair off, and something in the act of me accepting its inabilities made me happy. My mother had also cut all of her hair off, she was nearly bald and had dyed it almost every color before deciding she wanted locs. We were no strangers to locs—in Jamaica, they were everywhere, but they didn't always mean the same thing. For Rastafarians they were a covenant, and to us, they were just a hairstyle—another way to let our hair do what it does without us trying. Right before I left for college, my mother locked her hair, and it was marvelous. Immediately, I knew I wanted locs the same as hers—they were so undeniably breathtaking, that I was startled when she forbade me to do it. My mother was so liberal about my hair—there was never any hesitation in her allowance of my experimentation, so I didn't understand what changed in her and made her so rigid and indignant about me never having locs. Even more surprising than her outright refusal was her rationale—she said she wanted me to be eligible for jobs, and with locs they "wouldn't even let me work at the bank." I let her thoughts float in the air between us, and I let mine die on my lips, numb. I knew there was no bridge with enough range to join us in how we saw the world, so I disguised myself in silence to stay on her side, just this once. Two years later, I was devastated when I had no choice but to loc my hair. In its perm, it was thin and falling, but not the way my mother did in that picture; it came out in clumps with my fingers as I ran my hands through it, wishing it would fight to salute me one last time.

...

The Virgo Family

In 2018, Dale and Sherine's five-year-old daughter was denied the right to attend to the Kensington Primary School in St. Catherine, Jamaica, because her hair is locked. The public school claimed that her hair violates its institutional policy. At the school's orientation meeting, the principal told Sherine that children with locs are not permitted entrance for "hygiene" reasons—to purportedly "avoid outbreaks of lice." Though the court handed down an injunction allowing the girl to attend the school temporarily, Kensington's decision was ultimately upheld as constitutional, and the Virgos, officially denied, decided to homeschool their little girl.

...

Reading this story reminded me of the uncleanness I felt when my mother told me about her British-trained aunts' contempt for her own hair. For years, before I had my own locs, my mother refused to perm my hair, so she used a texturizer in it—loosening my curls but not straightening them. One Saturday my father took me to his sister's hairdresser, an Indian-Jamaican lady who straightened it all the way through. When he picked me up, he said, "This is the way I like your hair." That day my hair reminded me of his sister's daughters—it was not my hair. I wondered if he liked anything about me that was mine. I never asked.

...

I remember my time studying in South Africa fondly. But I remember less fondly the voice of my Indian-Zimbabwean thesis coordinator asking me if I would be washing my locs in my three-month stay. Too stunned to respond, I looked back at her, feeling the heaviness in my tongue paralyze me. She elaborated that the program had hosted Black female scholars before me who allegedly didn't wash their hair, and she gesticulated wildly while she described their stench. She waited for me to smile into complicity, betraying the mirroring in me that reminded her of them. I did. I had wanted her to believe me—that I was clean in spite of my locs—but my treason would earn me neither that classification nor my humanity, only the emptiness in acknowledging my own defeat. She flattened me, and I allowed it.

I never understood why all the Black girls in those schools in Durban had shaved their heads, when all the girls of other races got to keep theirs. I was told that it was to protect them from infestations of lice. They were dirty too.

The Lost Language of Tenderness

On my first day of school in Jamaica, I didn't know where I was going. I'd been to school before, but just getting dressed for this school was a whole new experience. Over my underwear, I pulled up a checkered, purple-and-white pair of bloomers, with a very noticeable elastic fastening presence around my waist, and the mid-point of my thighs. From the elastic, one more whimsical inch of fabric only served to frill its way around the circumference of each of my legs. The bloomers were a strange ligation. In my bloomers I looked like my body was a tube, and their elastic was my tourniquet, stopping the flow of all my internal elixirs so that inside of them, I was a swollen balloon. Those same purple-and-white boxes ran all over me, covering my uniform dress, which, without fanfare, looked like a sleeve that reached down to my knees and stopped suddenly, this time without the frills. Around my neck, I wore a white Puritan collar, with three small transparent buttons running down the center of my chest. The buttons laid atop a tie that was stitched onto my uniform and was also cut from the same purple-and-white grid. While I wore brown leather shoes and white socks with this same dress every day until I was ten years old, I will never forget my very first day in school. I was alone in my first-grade classroom. Half of the wall to the corridor was concrete, and the other half was a lattice of steel bars. I cried violently as I watched my mother's figure float away from me on the other side of that grillwork, but the most horrific sinking feeling I had that day came later when I saw my aunt walking toward the classroom to check on me, except by the time she came, I was no longer crying. I knew then that I had become one of them—full, Black native, inoculated against the weakness of feeling. My family wouldn't worry for me anymore because my aunt had seen that I could stuff my anguish like the flesh in my bloomers, and go numb.

...

My course to callousness was complicated and onerous. Before my first day of school in Jamaica, I had lived all six years of my life in the United States. I walked into a new world in that school building, with its jarring egg-green walls, the coldness of its shiny concrete floors, metal chairs, and wooden desks, accentuated by the unusual accents wafting over chests intentionally coated several times over with talcum powder. There were so many things I had never seen before. Prior to my first day, school meant reading corners, giant pillows, colorful carpets, glossy posters, and beautiful picture books. My teachers were different in Jamaica—they did not smile at me. Their eyes looked angry and remote, and I knew that if I was left with them, I'd get lost. My tears didn't move them and no one hugged me. I was made to sit, made to regulate myself, made to stop "giving trouble"—the trouble of my crying was disconcerting to them. I was terrified. On my first day of school, I lost the language of my tears, and long before, my teachers had lost the language of their own tenderness—we were all surrounded by loss. I walked through the doors and somehow my feelings became a public nuisance, not a private right. Among them, my right to feel and express didn't belong to me anymore—if I did that here, I was just a "naughty girl," not a sad one. They made me obedient, and I made my feelings to obey me—I made them go away. On my first day of school, I learned that a "good Jill" can make herself stop feeling or pretend that she does not feel. I didn't hit myself on the palm with two wooden rulers tied together as my teachers did, but I did push my pain inward in a way that felt just as violent as "Mr. Dickie." Sadness wasn't in our dissociative vernacular—at school we were obedient or we were punished for disturbing the unhealthy homogeneity we were never meant to escape. By my second day, I understood the purple boxes crawling all over me, crawling over all of us were there to remind us that we are not meant to be who we are. I often wonder, when my aunt looked into my eyes through the grillwork, could she see that my sadness was already gone for good?

...

In 2018, the U.S. Department of Labor released its *Findings on the Worst Forms of Child Labor* Report, indicating that even though 98.9% of the Jamaican population's children are going to school, a significant number of obedient children aged 5 through 14 are also silently "engaging in the worst forms of child labor." The US-DOL reports that "at the behest of parents or criminal leaders, referred to as 'dons,' [obedient children] are forced into commercial sexual exploitation. (1) Children also continue to be recruited by criminal organizations to engage in illicit activities, such as gang violence, guns and drug smuggling, and financial fraud, including lottery scamming (1; 13; 16). Child domestic workers may be subjected to domestic servitude, and some children are subjected to forced begging." The cost of being refused their feelings and thereby refusing to feel is that without feelings, we are less than human and can be made to do anything. If society fails to see every human as a feeling being, some humans will be made more vulnerable to abuse. The colonized society dehumanizes its children because it is a place in which humanity cannot survive.

Docile Black Breasts

I am milk chocolate brown. My undertones are red, and more often than not, my lipstick is of the darker variety. My hair is not curly, or wavy, but completely locked together. I am not small, and my voice is not soft. My laughter is a breathy deep staccato baritone that could be an audio-caricature of women at the market who sit with their legs wide open, skirts gathered in-between. I am a Black woman, and my Blackness has made an inscription on every facet of my being. I am a full Black being.

…

That Sunday on Amy's family boat, her aunts and uncles sailed with us. Her aunt was wispy thin, and seemed to me to be an underdeveloped woman. She asked Amy if my breasts were real. Her conceptions of my hypersexuality were trespassing on the family outing. I was 16, and they were White. The other Black bodies there were raising the main and steering us toward the wind. When we returned, and stopped over at the polo club, the whitewashed trunks of the palm trees warned me away from what was still, in truth, an imperial playground. **We** didn't go there. Inside of the property's plantation house, I could smell Black knees in the floor polish even though there only White feet dancing on the floor—and mine. Somehow in my own Black country, I knew my Black body, with its "exaggerated" breasts, did not belong here.

…

Mum Lacey was Amy's grandmother. She had a beachside apartment on the other side of the island. Driving there, I knew she was from a time that wouldn't welcome me inside of her home. She was watchful of me, and I hated her mouth. When Amy and I got into a fight, I screamed loud enough for my soul to lay bare, and our friendship couldn't survive the decibel. I wanted to desecrate the grounds and bring them all to their knees while I stood dancing with my breasts.

…

Black people are expected to remain in an unconditional and deferential politeness. They are trained to make themselves an apology. The politeness codifies that the Black person accepts he or she is not fully human and cannot present to society the full range of themselves. It is an attempt at civilizing the beast, and an affirmation of the beast's inherent brutality. The polite Black disarms the colonizer, assuring them of their obedience through obeisance. The willingness to adhere to arbitrary rules—albeit ones that had been designed to erase them—is tacit compliance with the colonizing system. Politeness operates as a permit system for safe passage in a colonized society; it communicates that the Black person is tamed and mastered. If unwilling to be polite, the Black person is castigated, remanded to the margins of society, and lambasted for the audacity of their impertinence.

By embracing the fury that was already feared in me, I rid myself of the tyrannical hold of colonizing decorum and respectability politics. I belted out of my rage and the structure that allowed me to remain in those White spaces with those White people crumbled beneath my feet. I knew what I was doing. The Black body is always vulgar in the eyes of the colonizer, so I allowed mine to embrace animation in every nuance of its frustration. I refused to mute or translate my indignation into a respectable surrender, knowing my transgression would banish me. This is the choice every Black being must make.

In her theoretical analysis of the Afro Caribbean woman's capacity to achieve "respectability" while guarding her own sense of "self-respect," sociologist Cecilia Green (2006) asserts that imposed cultural, structural, and historical imperatives for respectability contradict inherent notions of Afro Caribbean self-respect. The truth is *we* have to choose whether to remain docile on our knees, or dance on colonizing structures that will give way to our own collapse once we are truly standing.

As an example of this fierce and decolonizing self-respect, Usain St. Leo Bolt, a Black man from rural Jamaica, made a meteoric rise to stardom in August 2008 during the Olympics in Beijing, China. With unfavorable headwinds at the time of the sprint and an untied shoelace working against him, Usain devastated every other runner in the competition by setting a new world record without even running his hardest for the entire length of the race. Once he realized how far ahead of his competition he was, Bolt stopped running and began to jog, celebrating his victory untraditionally to the extreme delight of those whom he represented home in the Caribbean. Yet while Bolt was met with an international backlash for what was labeled poor sportsmanship, the Caribbean was awash with joy at the audacity of his excellence. In this moment, the world watched the unhappy meeting of European conventions of "respectability" and the Black expression of daring "self-respect." As expected, Bolt was rebuked for the boldness with which he loved himself. He displayed his full Black person without subjecting it to the smallness required for Blacks to be permitted passage. When interviewed, he offered in an assuring tone: "I wasn't bragging. When I saw I wasn't covered, I was just happy" (Tokyo2020, 2020).

Seven years later, while living in an upper-class neighborhood among White Jamaicans, Bolt was disparaged again, this time for not going "back where he came from." His White neighbor tweeted: "Between the bikes ... loud, horrid music, parties and screams, I honestly wish he would go back to where he came from. He's a horrible neighbor. I cannot wait to move" (Jamaica Observer, 2015). A third-party neighbor, who elected to remain unnamed, mentioned that the complaining neighbor also routinely hosted events that could be heard throughout the community. With news companies all over the world picking up the story, this time Usain St. Leo Bolt *respectably* surrendered—he simply did not respond.

Darkies Dancing

In my memory, when I started becoming aware of music, I would try to add loud, soulful, and unending vibrato runs to every song. It seemed to me that good songs always incorporated spontaneous, effortless artistry in this way. Soon that became attempts to harmonize with every note of every song, and without a musical ear to rely on, car rides with me were quickly very unpleasant. But at around 7 or 8 years old, I discovered dancing. I'd pop one of my mother's contemporary gospel albums into our oversized boombox, move the coffee table out of alignment with its permanent grooves in our sun-washed carpet, and just like that, my living room became a high-gloss dance studio. Hours felt like minutes as I diligently rehearsed my own choreography to eight counts of everything I'd seen that I could replicate. I loved to dance, and I did it every day, all day if I could. One year, my brother and I invited all of my mother's friends to our home for a surprise birthday party for her, and I was responsible for the entertainment—every item on our puff paint program offering was a dance by me. It was all the entertainment our budget could afford. 5, 6, 7, 8.

...

In school I had finally come of age to take Dance as an extracurricular activity, and the choice was a no-brainer. Ms. Campbell was fiercely angular with piercing almond eyes, and her muscles were magnificent. She also had a sharp tone; when she corrected you, you could feel her instructions impaling your tendons. Soon enough her disappointment in me was deadening, and dance classes would find me sullenly on guard against her next attack. I was confident in my ability to do the moves, but my memory failed me often and I couldn't remember the steps—I was a dancer too muddled to know what came next, so nothing ever flowed like real movement. She would bluntly tap my legs or push my arms, but even though I knew they were wrongly placed I didn't know where she wanted me to put them.

Every day I sank further into her quiet fury, and I didn't know how to make my way back to the surface. I didn't know how to fix myself for her, but Katherine never needed to. Her particular mix of Indo-African awarded her looser curls, longer plaits, fairer skin, and the unmistakable affection of Ms. Campbell, whose hue was a concentrated midnight. Some days I found myself so full of thoughts of Katherine there was no room left to think about dancing. This love of mine that stole away all of my days and nights in the living room now felt more like a stranger. I started to accept that Ms. Campbell would never marvel at my chest lifts and contractions unless I had Katherine's golden skin. I decided then that I would not love dance anymore, and I would not love Ms. Campbell. In my final performance with the dance troupe at the inter-school festival, I was on the left wing of the stage far enough over to dip behind the curtain without detection. But in this production, we were dancing to the spirited rendition of "The Lord's Prayer," performed by Mbongeni Ngema for the Sarafina soundtrack. At the time, I had never seen the singer or watched the movie, but I could sense those intonations were a clarion call for flat-backed girls with an unusual capacity for hinge and isolation like me. We danced what we felt in our bellies, and on that stage I danced my last dance so robustly that I breathed it out of me. I did not need my memory, or Katherine, or Ms. Campbell. I danced with Mbongeni.

At the very end, after we'd fluttered backstage and collapsed into a pile of heaving chests, red lips, and wrapped heads, Ms. Campbell locked her eyes in on me and marched toward me with a determination that felt like heat on my cheeks; even though I didn't turn to watch her, I could feel her narrowing approach. Her mouth smiled but her eyes did not as she announced to everyone that I had stolen the show, and she wondered where I had been hiding that performance all year. Katherine's solo lasted for more than half of our performance; I could feel Ms. Campbell's contempt for my audacity to lunge my way into significance from the choral line. I still did not look at her. I would not be beguiled by a woman who revered an aesthetic that neither she nor I could have, and I refused to allow my heart attachment to her approval for her affection—I knew the cost for my weight-bearing pigment would be extortionate.

…

My mother enrolled me with a ballet company led by two White women: one had a blonde bob and mild blue eyes, and the other, short curly brunette hair and a snarling mouth. Eleanor, the latter, owned the place. She was loud and severe, and Madeline was quiet and kind, but in a withering way I never fully trusted. I wondered if my mother hadn't noticed that everyone in the company was either White or very close to it. I noticed everyone's Whiteness though, and I always felt them noticing my dirty Black skin. In the changing rooms, I'd see them move their things away from mine—they tried diligently not to make skin-to-skin contact with the beast. If that wasn't enough, we were expected to wear uniform leotards, but instead my mother dressed me in the most unique variety of costumes, most of which were so ornate that they made it all but impossible to wear my required belt-and-wrap skirt. After every class, Eleanor and Madeleine would hold me back and scold me for my unruly hair that refused to make a bun, and my statement bodysuits. Even then I knew it was wrong for them to blame me for my mother's protest. My body has always been a protest.

…

In June of 2017, Rebekah Kebede (2017) wrote an article for *Marie Claire*, "Why Black Women in a Predominantly Black Culture Are Still Bleaching Their Skin: Investigating Deep-Rooted Ideals in Jamaica." Kebede, an Ethiopian woman whose own hue borders Whiteness, interrogates her 22-year-old subject, Jody Cooper. As Cooper reflects on her experience of bleaching her skin for nine consecutive years, she doesn't recall it as a conscious choice so much as an unavoidable reality: "When you black in Jamaica, nobody see you."

Beast of Burden

At the time, I was living in the United States and working as a teacher, but I had come home to Jamaica for the summer months. Tiffany had just moved back to Kingston from New Haven for good. She was fumbling her way through the Caribbean employment economy, and it was proving more difficult than any of us would have imagined. Along the way, she found Jesus, and decided to forgo her young adult dalliance with pansexuality and a notorious penchant for cannabis. The changes were unexpected, but I was suspicious of their practicability, so I remained vacantly watchful of her.

One day she asked me to accompany her to her church's small group meeting, and owing to my own convoluted relationship with the religious establishment at the time, I imprudently agreed. There is no official caste system that distributes admission to high society for the Jamaican public, but when you're among them, you can taste it in the air like the double agony of eating lemons: it starts with bitterness on the tongue and then swells into an eerily resonant vibrational pain in the triangle between your jaw, ears, and neck that lasts longer than planned. That familiar piercing feeling activates when the glands beneath your tongue and the parotid glands between your jaw and ears are triggered into overproducing saliva so that you can digest unusually tangy foods, but the tartness of Jamaican high society resists palatability by design, and in all these years I'm still yet to fully absorb and expel the vinegary mix of Tiffany's small group that day.

It was a microcosm—White men were meant to speak, and Black women were meant to listen acquiescently—but I defied the convention, and the consequences were explosive. The White man with whom I disagreed grew louder and louder, redder and redder, and the more he expanded his monstrous posture to swallow me whole, the more I locked into my position, methodically etching away at the credibility of his argument. Ironically, through his sweat and brawn, he was doggedly advancing the point that as a Christian he could be perfect, and I argued the contrary: that to follow Jesus is a humbling declaration that perfection is inherently beyond us, and in that acknowledgment, one is rendered completely dependent on the One who is. His oafishness appalled me, but more galling than his barbarianism were the pastors who sat quietly encircled, trapped in their high yellow caste just beneath his Whiteness. Tiffany's silence was also blaring, as the darkest among us, she likely thought none of us would hear her echoes from the lowest frequency of the hierarchy. Even in the car on the way home she was quiet. Numb to the residue of colonial civilizing missions and their psychological brutality, she was likely worried that I had disturbed the order of things, and her uneasiness sat between us. I accepted then that she would preserve her access to the institution by smiling and looking on from inside, even if it meant them building their empire on her back.

...

Colonizing missionaries established education as an institution in the Caribbean as thoughtfully as they did their religious systems. Built into the fabric of both institutions is the pervasive White supremacist silencing of the oppressed. Perhaps this explains why on January 22, 2021, the Brookings Institution (2021) released a brief on the epidemic of gendered violence in Jamaican schools (Kennedy, 2021). Girls, who fall into a lower caste in this hierarchical configuration, are being raped and assaulted in schools at alarming rates—especially between the ages of 13 and 17—and this is to say nothing of the emotional, verbal, and psychological abuse they suffer both within schools and their wider communities. Perhaps the riskiest and most compelling finding is how silent they are resolved to remain, in the ugly bargain for an education.

Ionie

We came to live in Jamaica when I was six years old, and moved straight into the house in which my mother was raised. To this day, I don't know which of the bedrooms used to belong to her—there was no nostalgic intimacy between my mother and that place. I think she imagined more for herself when she left the island, studying tirelessly into her twenties, and into her official certification as a Doctor of Dental Surgery, but being here again made her smaller, less of who she was before. Mockingly, she left her dental practice in the United States in pursuit of what she called "a better quality of life," but it seemed to me to be less than the life she wanted. I've heard before that people who speak multiple languages have different personalities in each idiom. My mother's nature changed in that way, but not along the lines of dialect so much as emplacement. In this setting, I relearned my mother, and much of who she was to me in our home was framed by Ionie.

Before I came to know Ionie, I had thought of my mother as my protector, but once she was with us, Ionie dutifully guarded my mother—without her, I would never have thought of my mother as someone who needed sanctuary. She had domestic responsibilities in our home, and soon after she joined us, my mother asked my father to leave. After that, we all watched my mother wither, and become an even more foreign version of herself. This strengthened Ionie's resolve to be loyal to her, and to this day they live in a quiet harmony alone—my mother and Ionie. Theirs is a type of symbiotic partnership, an agreement. For years, Ionie lived with her husband and only came to us on designated days, but when he passed away, she was offered shelter with my mother in a barter for menial household responsibilities. From it, my mother receives a type of loyal partnership—unconditional agreement, and the satisfaction of having her own sentiments exaggerated and mirrored back to her at every turn. In all her years with my mother, I've never seen Ionie with all three of her dimensions—she brings with her only the parts of use and interest to mother. She knows how to be with my mother without ever fully being there—the intricacy of her skill and the diligence of her dedication astounds me. She is masterful at the game, I've never seen her lose.

...

Shirley Pryce has been a vocal advocate for domestic workers, many of whom lost their positions in the COVID-19 pandemic, and have gone largely unsupported by the government of Jamaica in the wake of the crisis. Pryce, a former domestic worker who is now recognized by UN Women for her achievements in chairing the Caribbean Domestic

Workers' Network, recalled what it cost her to become three-dimensional while in her role: "I worked for a family of four in Kingston for nine years. I wanted to study and enrolled into evening classes. But I was a live-in domestic worker and my employers didn't think I should have any time for myself. When I came back from school at night, I found the door locked. I rang the doorbell; I knocked, but they didn't open the door. I slept in the dog house. This happened repeatedly" (UN Women, 2017). My mother once offered Ionie the opportunity to work her way up to becoming a dental assistant in her practice, but she declined. She told me later that she was too afraid.

The Talmers Syndrome

Nearly five decades ago there was a bank robbery in Stockholm, Sweden. Two men held four victims hostage for six long days and nights, but when the hostages were finally released, they vehemently refused to testify against their captors. In fact, instead they fundraised support for their kidnappers' legal defense team. Concomitantly, they had been threatened by their imprisoners, and completely reliant on them for survival. Something strange happened to these victims as a result—even though they were being held against their will on pains of death, they cultivated a deep sense of compassion for their captors. The slightest turn of kindness from their abductors had reshaped them toward emotional attachment. In the mental health field, they named this phenomenon of feeling positive feelings toward people who defile you 'Stockholm Syndrome.'

Twenty-nine years later, and 5,317 miles away, I was standing on very hot black pavement in Kingston. At 12 years old I could feel the heat coming up through the rubber soles of my black suede shoes, and I was at school. The shoes were always completely covered in dust, so distant from the way I imagined they looked on the shelves on which they were found in a store in America. I could only envisage it because I wasn't there. Summer school shoe shopping looked like me tracing a line around my foot on a piece of paper on the cold tile of our dining room floor, and then sending that sketch with my father to wherever he was going. When he came back, I'd have shoes, and that was the end of it. Everything seemed cleaner before it touched me, I was as dusty as the pavement in my mocking suede shoes, and debris climbed effortlessly up my socks and calves to camouflage itself in my skin. I felt stuck to that blacktop as I watched what I would later discover to be some loathsome variant of Stockholm Syndrome playing out right in front of me.

This time the assailant was Bryce Talmers. Because of his autism, he was always outfitted with a personal aide, a Black woman with green classes, short greasy hair, and a visceral displeasure stitched permanently into the furrows between her brows. One could never be completely sure what he understood of his surroundings, but he was unremitting in his determination to yell "IGNORANT NIGGERS" at us whenever he was so inclined. He was lily White, with raven hair, imposing eyebrows, and beady dark brown eyes. He was a puffy boy with no distinctive form, who somehow also managed to be incontrovertibly shaped like the letter S. His invectives, this time hurled at me, incensed my fury in the course of my walk to the cafeteria to buy a callaloo loaf, a personal box of Freshh orange juice, and a plantain tart. I stopped suddenly and fell still in the cloud of dust surrounding my shoes. I felt the heat coming up through the concrete, and flames swallowing my chest, and just as the tide of words were about to break ground from my lips, his band of protectors set their sights on me. They were all girls around my age, Black ones, who took it upon themselves to stand guard and police anyone who would take offense to his insults. Their weapons were shame and irrational anger, and they would unleash the full weight of their arsenal even if you simply deigned to be silently upset in the wake of what he'd said to you. To them, any agitation at Bryce was an unforgivable abuse.

I thought of drawing a line around his serpentine body, like I did my feet, and giving his silhouette to my father before realizing that to eliminate the problem, I'd also have to draw a line around the band of girls protecting him. I felt dizzy at the thought of it with the sun pelting down on my forehead, and beads of sweat gaining momentum as they ran into the creases of my back. I was resentful—I'd be damned if I stood to fight and lost favor with the last few girls who might have become my friends one day, and I'd be damned if I relented and walked away to get my food while his prejudice echoed from every step as my ugly shoes hit the gravel—each stride taking me closer to a meal I'd hate myself for. Bryce's aide was an adult, but she sat silent. I knew if I dared to react she'd grow even more grotesque. I chose to argue but incoherently, which amused them and gave them a strange combination of contempt and pity for me—I'd failed even to be worthy of the full force of their derision. I also walked away before fully standing my ground and stating my case—somehow I managed to lose the game in two ways instead of one. While walking away I heard Bryce's piercing crescendo, as he shouted "VIOLENCE" at the next casualty passing by. My shoes took turns rumbling "ignorant" (left foot) ... "nigger" (right foot) ... "ignorant" ... "nigger" ... "ignorant" ... "nigger" right up to the window, where I ordered twice as much food as I'd planned. I ate all of it alone in my shoes.

Mulatto

The word "mulatto" is derogatory. It is a half-caste classification for Afro European people. The regions of the world that boast the highest concentration of them are South America, Southern Africa, North America, and the Caribbean. Within those regions, the country that ranks highest is Brazil, and not far behind in seventh place is Jamaica. Though to be mulatto is essentially to be a mix of more than one thing, most of the mulattos I encountered early in my life were in hysterical pursuit of distilling the mixture of themselves into the singular crowning achievement of passing into Whiteness. The casualty of cutting away their own Blackness was vile enough to make me grimace on cue whenever we crossed paths.

Enigmatically, I couldn't quite articulate exactly how they were different from me growing up but somehow, I could spot them effortlessly. I didn't know why. The thought had crossed my mind more than once that they all convened and agreed on a shared agenda for ensuring we Blacks knew that they were not the same as us, but I was never able to confirm it. I rarely saw them, but when I did they would always be together. Mostly, I'd see them once a year in the annual Miss Jamaica World beauty competition—nearly every contestant had golden skin, was rail thin, and had long wet hair that typically fell in ringlets, unless straightened out to do otherwise. They sounded different, they looked different, and they kept to themselves. This worked for me, until I had the unfortunate experience of having an OB-GYN appointment with Dr. Sally Arthurson.

Even though I was a young adult when I finally went to see her, I'd known her indirectly for years. When I was younger, the mulatto girls I knew called her Aunt Sal, but for me it was strictly Dr. Arthurson. I understood my place in the agreement—my parents were well off enough for us to know of each other, so she would greet me if the situation absolutely required it, but my hue would always deny me the evolving intimacy that naturally grows between people over time. We were not people to each other; I was the cancer she was cutting out of her own body and that Blackness was known to be virulent. I felt pity for her, as I thought she may well manage to carve out her own Blackness, but I knew she'd never be fully White. At best, she'd be half of a person in the end, with no true place but among other fractured mulattoes, scattered in their own journeys to complete a fool's errand. History had gotten the best of them, and they were lost.

After college, I lived for years in Washington, D.C. teaching in a public school. Every year I'd spend most of my summer months in Jamaica. On one unusual trip, my mother spontaneously booked me a visit with Dr. Arthurson. I had something akin to a phobia about seeing an OB-GYN, so I never saw one, but I decided my young adulthood would be a good time to tackle that dread head on, and I agreed. The visit began with terse, sharp questioning that stunned me into instantly remembering that I did not belong there. I had forgotten the rules after years being away, encountering many mixed people, mulattos included, who had no designs on cutting the Blackness out of themselves. But nothing had changed for this particular group in Jamaica, or Dr. Arthurson. She snarled at my answers, openly conveying her misgivings about my alleged sexual inexperience. After all, bodies like mine were born only for illicit pleasure and suffering that chestnut eyes like hers shouldn't have to see—Jezebels. Her contempt filled the examination room, her mouth releasing airy sounds intent on my derision. She repeated my sentences with an exaggerated American drawl, openly reprimanding me for trying to present as if I were an American.

My ability to live in the United States had deeply upset her. In essence, I had disturbed the order of things. It seemed she was worried that I was not seeing her with the necessary deference of the previous unspoken agreement. Her distress was physically violent to my body—she gave all of my irrational fears plausibility as, one by one, she did the things I was most afraid a doctor might do to me without announcement. When she was done I felt brutalized. I had smiled my way through her preliminary insults hoping she wouldn't violate me, but my self-belittlement was futile, and she did it anyway. Inexplicably, even after she was done I kept smiling and nodding like a half-wit, all the way out of her office. I didn't leave without thanking her at least three times. Imperiously, without once looking me in my eye, she had hollowed me of my dignity, returning me pointedly to my rightful place. I wondered how even with all of my Blackness still in tow, the curse the mulatto carries is still mine to bear.

The Prize You Don't Win

The moment I saw him, I was his. Only one-year older, his skin was a blessed mix of hickory and burnt umber, and his lips a wildly roguish charcoal coffee. He was confection for my eyes, and when they couldn't see him, my mind would etch out a fresh rendering for me on demand.

He was intoxicating, I had never felt like this before. In all my 13 years, I had no inkling I could be so taken as I was with Calvin.

For the most part, I admired him from afar. For two years, I skulked in the shadows, silently finding ways to be near enough to hear his laugh escape the space between his fingers while he threw his head backwards in a mindless roar of joy. I'd carefully trail him with my eyes under the cloak of the artifice of distraction, studying him so earnestly that I knew the strange cadence of his speech. I could pick his words out of the air before he said them—needless to admit, I was hopelessly smitten. But apart from one desperate attempt to be seen by him—when I joined a co-ed sports team he was a member of for two practices—I remained swallowed up in a quiet restraint for as long as I knew him.

When I was 14, I discovered he may have always felt my eyes watching him. One rainy afternoon, under the concrete cover of the school hallway, he brushed by me, and when I looked up, he had my left palm between his thumb and index finger lazily … effortlessly. I was paralyzed, as the hush of the vacant campus grounds closed in on me, and my eyes began to glaze. He leaned downward toward me, in that signature diagonal posture I'd come to idolize, and softly he kissed me on my lips and walked away. I stood stunned, immobile, wondering if I'd just had a waking fever dream, while my mind pulsated recklessly, pushing heat through my ears. My tongue wagged around my mouth sorting through the cotton of my breath. I didn't know why it happened to me, but I learned to be grateful for kisses that were taken before I'd thought to give them. I learned from the one I wanted to kiss me most.

That same year, I'd gotten into a fight, and my mother sent me to another school. She'd always said that although my school was rated the best in the island, all the children felt entitled there. She didn't want me becoming one of them. I never said goodbye to him, and I never thought I'd see him again, but I was about to turn 16 when I did. I wanted to give him an invitation to my sweet 16 party, so I summoned the courage to get his number, and I called. He remembered me and offered to come to my house to pick up the invitation. I thought fondly of the exchange and looked forward to seeing him. I wore a pink-and-white striped summer dress and pink sandals to the gate when he arrived. I walked out to hand him the invitation, not thinking he expected to come in, but when he did I was elated at the thought of spending time with him. This exhilaration coupled with my impulsive anxiety intensified as the engine of his ride revved and pulled away. What would we talk about until they returned? I focused all of my attention on maintaining a dispassionate affectation while sweat washed over me. I walked him to my backyard for the first stop on a tour that would end on my verandah, but once I turned to look up from dodging the rotting mangoes in the grass, his lips were on mine again. This was a pleasant surprise—I was happy in his arms. I was a princess in my mid-weight, cotton A-line, pale pink-and-white stripes, and I was about to pop my pointed foot like a damsel when I felt his hand suddenly traveling up my dress.

This time, my shock ricocheted me violently away from his chest. My mind was confused. Didn't he know that ours was a timeless kind of love? An unrequited tale for the ages that could only end in houses, and children, and porches, and rocking chairs? Why did I feel so common … so carelessly trespassed by the beautiful chocolate boy I was sure I wanted kissing my perfectly cocoa cheeks? I was sure I was a princess, so why was he touching me like I was a Jezebel? Was Jezebel a Jezebel? Are there any Jezebels or is that just the name we use for girls who look like me, even when we think we're something else? My mind ran on, but I knew well enough to keep my mouth smiling, even if my heart no longer felt indebted. I had started my descent into invisibility, stammering on, and smiling slyly, I muttered something clumsy about "not yet" and "being a virgin." He took one breath deep into his stomach to say what I'd hoped he'd been waiting to say for the last five years: "Shauna" … my name was still decadent in his mouth. "That's not an accomplishment, you were born that way. You don't get a prize." And I didn't.

The Anonymous, Invisible Afro Caribbean American

The first Census survey was issued in the United States in 1790 to take account of who was present in the United States of America. In that first year, only 13 states were counted, but in its most recent iteration in the year 2020, the count included 50 states in addition to Puerto Rico, American Samoa, the Commonwealth of the Northern Mariana Islands, Guam, and the U.S. Virgin Islands (Pew Research Center, 2020). In the Census, the people in the United States have always fallen into select categories. In 1790, they were "Free white males, Free white females," "All other free persons," and "Slaves." Over time, "Slaves" became "black," which then became "Negro" and "African American," and now "Black" and "African American." Still there is no trace of Afro Caribbean Americans present in the US Census. In a way, it means we remain not fully present in the United States.

Though the option "Black" is present, and does in fact accurately envelop Caribbean Americans of African descent, the categorization is the same selection as "African American." Consequently, there can be no disaggregation of the data that specifically offers an account of us. We are still waiting for existence. This conflation of "Black" and

"African American" fails us twice over. Once in name, as the panoply of Blackness, broadly defined, collapses clumsily into the specific "African American" designation which renders us an anonymous entity—always guests, only visiting both the country and the category. Twice in number, as the established function of the U.S. Census will never really count us, because there is no way to count an unnamed people. We are invisible. How do you value what you will not name and cannot count?

The sitting Vice President of the United States, Kamala Harris, was born of two immigrant parents. Her mother, Shyamala Gopalan Harris, was born in modern-day Chennai, Tamil Nadu, India, formerly the Madras Province of British India. After migrating to the United States at 19 and making this country her home, she became "Indian American" in identity and "Asian Indian" on the Census. This fortune, however, was never extended to her father, Donald Harris, an economist born in Browns Town in St. Ann, Jamaica. He has lived to read the letters of his name etched into the annals of history—"H-A-R-R-I-S"—and seen them framed as a landmark, one in which he still remains ... uncounted. Vice President Harris was sworn in and jubilantly celebrated as the first female Vice President, the first Black Vice President, and the first South Asian American Vice President. Yet there is no confession that the mention of "Harris" is an echo that traces back for generations to a small town in St. Ann in Jamaica. There is no name for us. Even the history we make is taken away.

Mule

For the first six years of my life, I lived in Beltsville, Maryland with my mother, father, and brother. When I was six years old, my father was offered a position at the University of the West Indies, so we moved to Jamaica for him to take it. Every year thereafter, we traveled back and forth: to Florida to see my grandmother, to New York to see my aunt, and to one place a year we'd never been before to see the world. Air travel was an unhappy companion of mine, a necessary evil. I hated the plane's take-off process, and I'd keep my CD player going even after being asked to power down my electronics so it could lull me into sure sleep before the wheels of the aircraft left the ground. I traveled so often that before I was ten, I was already traveling as an unaccompanied minor, making connections in crowded airports to navigate my way to my next home away from home.

As a pre-teen, I developed an irrational fear of escalators, after having ridden them comfortably for as long as I could remember. There was something about the height of them, and my imagination that one day a loose thread from the frayed hem of my bellbottoms could catch, and soon my pants would pull me into the mincer to be pulverized. I'd make it to the steel plate just before the first mechanized step—which would already be ascending or descending without me—and something about losing the choice to stop it from going became more frightening for me than missing my flight. Those traveling days filled me with an anxiety I'll not soon forget, and I will spare you the details of what emerged to be an absolute anguish about airport and airplane bathrooms. Eventually, I learned to maneuver my way around my own neuroses so that I would be able to see all the places and faces my heart desired, wherever they were.

Something changed when I was in college, but this time it wasn't me. I'd developed a deep appreciation for study abroad, so I'd leave my campus in Richmond, Virginia for summers and even semesters at a time to study in Europe and the African continent. Without announcement though, travel started to get harder for me in an inexplicable way. Customs officers turned the stamped pages of my passport more slowly, snarling at me about how much I "got around." What used to be a simple cursory viewing of my signed travel documents became laced with thinly veiled suspicion, and eventually grew to what could only reasonably be classified as latent interrogation. In order to study abroad as much as I did, I took very heavy course loads when I was stateside. One particular semester was so taxing that my hair started to fall out, so I decided to change my straightly processed tresses into tightly wrapped locs. I didn't know at the time that this hairstyle choice would signal to airport security that, without reservation, mine was a body they could violate. I was pulled by "random selection" in every airport screening line, and even invited to do cavity searches in dark, hidden rooms. I was grateful for one Cuban teacher I had in the ninth grade who had mentioned, as an aside, a turning point she had experienced in her travels. Once, airport security had told her they would strip search her, but she evaded the breach by announcing loudly that she knew her rights and several people in the press. Years later, during my own travails while traveling, I have pulled this line out of faded memory while in the throes of the shame of these requests, and sometimes it has saved me…sometimes.

Tools

In Jamaica, after the sixth grade we leave preparatory school and go straight into high school. And for me, that transition was an extraordinary one. The lift of absolutely everything was nearly too heavy to bear. In my new school, I was still smarting from the abrupt separation from my best friend. Prior to it—to put it mildly—if she was the hand, I was the glove. When she had just arrived to our preparatory school as a transfer student, she had her pick of all of us for friendship. We had all known each other for as long as we could remember, and when she appeared in the fourth grade—all legs, and bright eyes—every one of us lined up dutifully for the chance to be her friend. Years later, right before we left for high school, in a last-ditch desperate frenzy to seal our allegiance permanently before we departed, I told her family that my mother had cancer in her finger. She did not, and when our friendship fizzled, I was at least relieved not to have to conjure up some miraculous recovery or the other. My desperate scrambling plans to keep us together had failed and we went our separate ways—her, to another line of girls beaming to be friends, and me, to a somewhat less promising absence of prospects.

Though I didn't make friends quickly, in almost no time at all I had a mortal enemy in Algebra. I had always hated Mathematics, but Algebra may as well have been taught in Cantonese—I couldn't make heads or tails of it. My teacher's eyes were hyperbolic, so globular and bulging that I spent most of the class gawking at their severity. Not to be outdone, her melodious Trinidadian inflections kept my ears buzzing to a piercing pitch. But nothing was so stunning as when she asked me a question, and I stood dumbly among my peers while she belted my name in disapproval—loudly enough for the entire block of classrooms to tune in for my ambivalence. She was angry, and my senselessness infuriated her reliably—class after class. No one batted an eye when she debased me; after all, being dressed down by the adults we knew was par for the course for us. They had decided that the only way to truly prepare us for the future to come was through cruelty and shame. In the end, I never learned the math—but the cruelty and shame, I mastered. Soon, I too was at the top of my lungs hurling invectives at anyone who didn't know what I thought they ought to. I also didn't make any friends.

Laundry for One

Owing to the fact that much of the Jamaican labor economy is domestic in nature, there are absolute yet unspoken rules that govern relations with people referred to as "the help." One can expect to be addressed everlastingly as "Miss, Mrs., Dr., or Mr.," and in return, should offer a kind of quarters of the home to the individuals in their service. Beyond view and with sufficient distance from the other residential rooms, stripped of the niceties enjoyed by the rest of the home, there ought to be a bedroom and bath, broadly defined, that none of the house residents use, clean, or service. These accommodations belong to "the help," but only so far as the frisky and boisterous children of the home will allow it, since they are typically allowed to traipse in and out of those private lodgings at their whim—after all, this is **their** house.

Though I can easily identify some general conventions of house service across Jamaica, there are some aspects of it within my experience that I've been too ashamed to inquire about beyond my own home. When we were 8 or 9 years old, our underwear was separated from the rest of the wash, and we were given basins, and blue soap, and taught to wash our own intimates. I made it a personal mission to get good enough at washing mine that I could make the same masterful scrubbing sound as Ionie. Skilled hands produced a distinct squirt and squelch while they washed, and I was determined to have them—I practiced until the bulging thenar eminence at the base of my thumb was rubbed raw and thin, and the lines disappeared from my hand's translucence. Over the years, if I strained to hear it, I might be rewarded with a faint splashing noise from time to time, but I never heard the diligent smacking and swishing that I had doggedly worked in expectation of. Over time, another thing I noticed was that in our adolescence, my brother's unmentionables went back into the regular wash with everyone else's clothes, but neither mine nor my mother's ever would. I came to understand that learning the sound was less about coming of age, and more about my unacceptably dirty Black woman body. "The help" could be made to suffer many indignities, but nothing so extreme as washing the intimates of a full-fledged woman body. After all, what could be dirtier than a Black woman—within the quarters or without.

Parapraxis

"Nora … NORA!" she would belt that name several times over and with increasing urgency—often for far longer than she cared to—before I would remember that she was talking to me. My name, of course, is not Nora, so it always took me some time to register that mine was the attention she was beckoning. My Aunt Nora had lived in America, so of course it was curious that her name was being repeated over and again, echoing off of the polished floors of a modest den at the back of our house in Kingston. It never surprised me, though, my grandmother said it so often around me that it alloyed into the rising orchestra of lizards croaking, and crickets chirping that was always seeping into my hearing from our backyard. It was really my grandmother's backyard by right, that was the ominous thing about our house—I was living my childhood in the house in which my mother had lived hers. Oddly, we never talked about that fact; in truth, to this day I don't even know which of our bedrooms belonged to her. Recreating the lives lived there in the past that were now being relived with me was an involuntary work that was incessantly taxing to my imagination. Sometimes I wondered if when my grandmother visited us in her old home, she was retrospectively re-touching her own past life, or taking a present account of what we were making of ours. Perhaps that's why it never startled me when she called me her daughter's name. No doubt, she would have sat mixing Christmas cakes with her in much the same way in this same room eons ago. I couldn't tell, and some knowing I never fully understood always kept me from asking, so instead I looked back at her and replied, "Yes, Grandma."

My grandmother had two girls—Nora, the younger of the two, was not my mother. It often struck me as peculiar that my grandmother never inadvertently called me my mother's name. She always called me Nora. When my mother heard her do it, she would quip that my grandmother called her Nora, too, but to this day I've never heard it. Of the two girls, my mother had fairer skin and longer hair, and my grandmother was known to call her "mi pretti dawta" (my pretty daughter). My grandmother's own skin, like Nora's, was a somber ebony; they both also donned short, spritzed curls that never touched their necks. I never really knew Aunt Nora for myself as a child, but I was told that like me, she "had a lot of lip" and was always getting into trouble—this was quite unlike my grandmother's "pretti dawta," who I was also told never did. I assumed the likeness that led to the enigma of my misnaming had more to do with who I was than what I looked like since I look more like my mother than my aunt, and I recognized almost instinctively that I certainly did not act like a "pretti dawta" the way I observed my mother to. I was not fragile, tender, deferentially obedient, or perpetually in need of help, and I begged for the bantu knots, known then to me as "chiney bumps," that were only an inside hairstyle for "pretti dawtas." Not least of all, without much effort it was easy to discern that my temperament was uncannily similar to my father's, who did not subscribe to the compulsory extolling of "pretti dawtas" meant to elevate them to some high artifice from which they could not be found out as lacking, or even in some instances, wrong altogether. Alas, I was too much of a disappointment to become a "pretti dawta." In fact, I may have been a threat to the entire institution. So I concluded provisionally that this was why my grandmother never called me my mother's name—in her disillusionment, she demoted me to the caste of "badly behaved" girls with midnight skin, and when she slipped into moments of parapraxis, she would even call me Nora. For some time I was her only granddaughter, so I could not be sure of this theory, but soon enough Aunt Nora had a daughter of her own—a pure, higher yellow than any of us, with almond eyes, and looser curls that made for longer tresses. Aldith was innately kind, and mild, and in the orchestra of my hearing I almost missed it the first day my grandmother appointed her "mi pretti granddawta" … almost.

Planned Obsolescence

My father's name is Lennox, but everyone in his family called him Barry. I'd asked enough times to understand why he'd earned the name not to ask again, but the answers never satisfied me. He was sort of a mythical creature in that way—everyone seemed to have legendary memories with him that lit up their faces in the most wholehearted way in the retelling. In one anecdote, they talked about him driving a tractor before he was six years old. In another affair, as a young boy his mother had taken him to the doctor, and when he'd heard he was meant to be subject to being injected in his rear, he turned to his mother and said "Come, Mama," instructing her to meet him at the car, where they both assuredly and unceremoniously headed home. As he aged, this certitude followed him into boarding school, where he met another youngster who made the wrong joke—Barry then moved him out of his room by abruptly dumping his suitcases over the second-floor railing, including all of his clothes. As a young adult, he graduated with some degree or another in the United States and received a trophy for distinction—some sort of genius award that he scarcely wanted, and definitely did not keep, so it lived with his sister in the hills in Kingston. That was the thing about Lennox, his absoluteness was almost the stuff of fiction.

After 11 years, my parents' marriage collapsed in on itself, and my father was swiftly ejected in a conversation for which I happened to be present in their bathroom. In true Barry-form, I decided then that if he left, I would go with him. Ironically, I was only six and had yet to hear any of these stories about my father. I suppose that mettle was in me, passed down to me, and when called on, it found no hesitation. Almost as quickly as he'd left our home, I, too, was gone. For a year and change, Barry and I were on our own to face the world. In spite of being separated from my mother and brother, we were not unassisted. I spent a great deal of time on my weekends with my cousins, and during the week, Arden did the cooking and cleaning in our home. One day Arden had to leave us, but no sooner did I meet Vantrice, and when she went away, Mrs. Riley took her place. This was not unusual, as all of the houses I knew intimately in Jamaica would endure this carousel of domestic economy workers until finding the just-right fit. This is why I was so surprised when Mrs. Riley's leaving was announced to me so gravely. At first I understood that

I would be going back to my mother's to spend the weekend while the matter of the next appointee was sorted, but the weekend turned into weeks, and weeks into months, and months into years, and here we are decades later and I am still yet to return. I couldn't help but wonder at the arbitrariness of the arrangement; somehow I was gone as quickly as I'd arrived and the lionhearted antics of Barry never materialized on my behalf. Perhaps instead, embedded in his plan was that a girl at my age ought to be with her mother rather than a parade of maternal figures who were only paid to clean his home. I suppose I'll never know—there are so many things that daddies and daughters never say.

References

Boyce-Davies, C. (2002). *Black women, writing and identity: Migrations of the subject*. Routledge.

Brookings Institution. (2021). Gender-based violence in primary schools: Jamaica. Brookings.edu. www.brookings.edu/research/gender-based-violence-in-primary-schools-jamaica/

Fanon, F. (2007). *The wretched of the earth*. Grove/Atlantic.

Green, C. A. (2006). Between respectability and self-respect: Framing Afro-Caribbean women's labour history. *Social and Economic Studies, 55*(3), 1–31. www.jstor.org/stable/27866468

Jamaica Observer. (2015, June 9). "Jinx," Bolt, and the power and danger of social media. Jamaicaobserver.com. www.jamaicaobserver.com/editorial/-Jinx---Bolt-and-the-power-and-danger-of-social-media_19110228

Kebede, R. (2017, June 21). Why Black women in a predominately Black culture are still bleaching their skin: Investigating deep-rooted ideals in Jamaica. *Marie Claire.* www.marieclaire.com/beauty/a27678/skin-bleaching-epidemic-in-jamaica/

Kennedy, D. (2021, January 22). Gender-based violence in primary schools: Jamaica. Brookings.edu. www.brookings.edu/research/gender-based-violence-in-primary-schools-jamaica/

Pew Research Center. (2020). What census calls us. www.pewresearch.org/interactives/what-census-calls-us/

Tokyo2020. (2020, June 27). Bolt strikes in Beijing in 2008. Tokyo2020.org. https://tokyo2020.org/en/news/bolt-strikes-in-beijing-2008

UN Women. (2017, April 10). From where I stand: "I slept in the dog house because I wanted to go to school." UNWomen.org. www.unwomen.org/en/news/stories/2017/4/from-where-i-stand-shirley-pryce

2 Disappearing

I investigate the phenomenon of the "disappearing self" by examining the interiority of the Black subaltern to discover how components of the subjectivity disappear. Existentialist philosopher William Barrett (1984) explains the notion of disappearance as the reabsorption of a writer into their literary work, or the vanishing of one "individual aesthetic voice" into a "desubstantialized" "free-floating matrix of signs." I broaden Barrett's conception of disappearance beyond reabsorption into literature to signify the dissolution, diffusion, and vaporization of the subaltern subjective self, which is an exacting prerequisite to gain full access to Anglo-supremacist society. When the subaltern is desubstantialized from their authentic form, they are then eligible to be reabsorbed into society in an acceptably compliant and submissive configuration of self. Once dissolved in this way, the subaltern—as they were—no longer exists. I offer several accounts of disappearance to signify moments of trespassing beyond the limits issued to all Black subalterns—psychologically, emotionally, physically, intellectually, interpersonally, and societally—and the gatekeeping that ensues to control and curtail those freedoms as a consequence. The subaltern is only allowed into society so much as they will comply with allowing parts of themselves to disappear.

In these accounts of contending with desubstantialization in order to elude disappearance, I address the implications for the Black subaltern's ability to perceive themselves as feeling beings, conscripts of respectability, the mutilation of Black bodies and psychic space, the liability of trust for Black subalterns even as a precondition for survival, the conflation of accomplishment with neo-indentured servitude, the slipping away of Black subaltern subjectivity that seeps out unintended, the weathering of the Black subaltern body, the prefiguration of pathological shame, and the compounded misogynoir-related trauma that results in the reabsorption of the Black subaltern self through integrated

DOI: 10.4324/9781003226802-3

subhumanity. If we allow ourselves to be as Black as we are, they will drown us in the darkness. If we refuse to be as Black as we are, they will make us disappear.

Trauma Is Not What We Called the Things that Happened to Us

We thought Kerensia was being melodramatic the week her father pulled out a gun on her mother in their bedroom, and Kerensia told her boyfriend she was planning to kill herself.

We thought Kay was a tart after her father left her mother and started another family; when she never saw him again, she started kissing all of the boys and talking about sex.

We thought Aisha was cosmopolitan when we learned that her trip from the Middle East to Jamaica—purportedly for vacation—was actually a permanent move. We envied the adventure even though we knew her family had absconded in the night and she never had the chance to say goodbye to all the people she would likely never see again on the other side of the world.

We thought Kimone was just low-born when her step-father moved her mother and sisters into the basement to make room for his new girlfriend, and she ended up having a baby with a druglord.

We thought Tye was an egomaniac when her uncle touched her and she started having sex with all of her friends' boyfriends before declaring herself a lesbian.

We thought Caryl was a fraud when, after she found out her mother had been sleeping with her boyfriend, she started stealing people's money and disappearing for months on end.

We thought a lot of things about ourselves and each other, but since we knew we weren't the sort of people who felt, we'd just accuse each other and laugh to keep away the silence.

Ad Hominem

In 2006, I was on my own for the first time in my life. I had left Jamaica for college in the United States, and while this was a major step for me, something far more staggering was happening back at home—for the first time in history, Jamaica had elected a female Prime Minister: The Most Honourable Portia Lucretia Simpson-Miller.

She campaigned under the distinctive slogan "Come to Mama," a nod to the many years she had committed to public service in which she was known to all of us as "Mama P." She was only the third woman to serve as head of government in the Anglophone Caribbean, and her allure was undeniable. With unmistakably rich deep brown skin, a past of humble beginnings which she never denied, and an uncanny ability to "talk with crowds and keep her virtue" and "walk with kings" without losing "the common touch" (Kipling, 1895), Mama P was a force to be reckoned with among the Jamaican proletariat. Throughout her work, Mama P's most pre-eminent virtue was her uncompromising commitment to the poor. It meant that when she spoke, she spoke to them, when she fought, she fought for them, and what she threw herself into was primarily in their service. In spite of her ranking as one of the "100 Most Influential Persons in the World" in Time Magazine (Jamaica Observer, 2012), she was still sufficiently second-class to be an easy target to the more traditional political elite—she did not and would not fit in. Her critics were relentless, never missing an oppor-tunity to conclude that she was unsuited for the position because she was of low birth, wanting in both respectability and education.

Though all politicians can be counted on like clockwork to pander to the poor by speaking Patois during their rallies, PM Simpson-Miller would finesse her way into and out of the lexicon at will. In one particularly memorable instance, she had responded to government overspending allegations with an uncommonly colorful diatribe: "Don't draw my tongue and don't trouble this girl, because I don't fraid a no man, no gyal, nowhere!" (Cooper, 2011).

High society was stiflingly flustered and up in arms, and the condem-nation of her vulgarity came in like a flood. It was clear to me then that Mama P and I were learning a very similar lesson—if I kept my blond braids, and she maintained her indiscrete nature, all we'd ever be was crude and inferior.

Even I Didn't Believe Me

For as long as I've been alive, people have always referred to my mother and father using their doctoral titles. I've never known them any other way. I should note here that there is a sort of forced formality in the Caribbean that has also dictated that in professional settings, and well beyond them, one is never without their title. In practical terms, this means that outside of our family, I've never heard anyone refer to my parents using their first names. This had a strange effect on me in my youth, since I found myself to be conclusively mediocre in every meaningful area of my life—at the time the areas of significance for me were singing, dancing, schooling, and sport, and I underwhelmed across the board. To be found wanting meant to me that I might be the first Myers to fall short of the crowning victory of a doctoral title. Thankfully, I was wrong about myself, and I would add that several teachers and admirable figures in my life were wrong about me, too. I was in fact able to be called Dr. Myers, though by that time I was Dr. Knox. A funny thing happened though—I never moved on from the feeling that I was only reaching for the title, even when it was mine. At first I thought I was engaging the requisite deference and self-deprecation masquerading as humility that is required for likeability in the contemporary age. Here in the developed world, first names abound, so I thought I'd show just how secure I was in my title by discarding it altogether. But on the rare occasion I did choose to use it, I found it would not sit in people's mouths. They would avoid addressing me altogether, or strip me of it, violently, without announcement. I'd see people become incensed when I dared to use it on myself and asked to be acknowledged in it. There was something about calling me Dr. Knox that they didn't believe, and neither did I.

Residue

If slave women were as strong as their male counterparts, they were worked just as hard and flogged just as mercilessly. Generally, both men and women were whipped, typically with select elements for emphasis, perhaps to avoid the indelicacy of the ordeal in some way. Corporeal punishment was designed to train slaves on the boundaries of acceptable behavior. The practice was so widely conventional that mutilation came to be an expectation for Black bodies. In most Caribbean families, the custom continues with a persistent orthodoxy, as slave descendants insist in its efficacy and even boast about their own abilities to withstand the most severe beatings. It seems an unintended consequence of being lashed in order to learn "right from wrong" is that these thrashings are then visited in turn on one's spouse, children, and even peers that transgress one's moral expectations. Unlike the animals, who when switched become tame, we have become bewitched by violence. We think back on sordid tales about our grandmothers sending us out into their farms to find thorny bushes that they then used to tear into our flesh, and we laugh at our terror and call it the good old days. We say that the discipline made more of us because the reach of our mutilation extends beyond our bodies, and violence is all we know.

The Parts I Kept for Myself

The way I said "schedule" as if there were no "c"—like I had been doing all my life—drew curious responses, so I kept it for myself.

The way I would throw myself to the ground in a completely uninhibited fit of laughter while stitched into the contractions of an uproarious merriment as I had always done ever since I was a little girl made them nervous about what I might do next, so I kept it for myself.

The way I browsed lavishly through the hair catalogue, thinking only of what I wanted to do next, transitioning seamlessly from flips with blonde tips to maroon pixie cuts made them spellbound with contempt, so I kept it for myself.

The way I savored organ meats like kidneys and livers and longed for them at breakfast time made me alien, so I kept it for myself.

The way I transposed the subjects and objects of my sentences and defaulted to negative sentence structures left a hollow pause at the end of my attempted transmissions, so I kept it for myself.

The way I approached any human as if we were both normal and knew nothing about each other made them grimace at my audacity, so I kept it for myself.

In truth I scarcely have the things I've kept for myself anymore. I don't think I was keeping them.

Dying of Survival

I am told that survivalists believe that the most indispensable commodity for subsistence and existence in the end is trust. In fact, researcher Malcolm Gladwell subscribes to what he calls the Truth Default Theory (2019), which posits that humans are so reliant on implicit trust, that no higher order activity can proceed without its presumption. This implicit trust is so commonplace that we acknowledge its presence as assumption, and without the assumption of memory, understanding, and application, the superior faculties of analysis, evaluation, and creation are all but an impossibility. What does this mean for us, whose implicit trust led us to be caged and traded like livestock for more than four centuries? What do we assume now that our naïve notions of humanity left us whipped, shackled, hanged, beaten, burned, mutilated, branded, raped, separated from our children, and imprisoned? What are we to make of all of the disappearing Black female bodies that never make the news, and all of the slain Black bodies that do? We are fighting to trust a world that has never been trustworthy for us in order to survive, only to die a psychic death of the soul day after day, or worse, die the physical death we could have avoided had we leaned into our baser instincts not to trust at all. We die because we do not trust, and we die because we do.

At Fourteen

Beloved Shauna,

By now you are fourteen, and you would have settled yourself into the idea that love is illusive and very difficult to come by. Indeed, the world has not loved you well—or at all really—and the people in it who do have determined to hurt you before it does to protect you from the shock of coming into the awareness of that grimy reality alone. They have designs on stripping away from you every place you've designated safe, to convince you never to feel safe again. In any other world this would be a cruel undertaking, but in this one it is mandatory—you are not safe, so feeling safety can carry with it lethal threat.

The whole thing is a ghastly business so you'll no doubt set your sights on more sophisticated places, where you imagine people will be kinder to you because they have a more cultivated understanding of life as a project, with purpose and adventure. You'll arrive to new worlds only to discover the cost of admission is dissolution into a caste of primates just shy of human—perhaps apes. The invisible debris of chattel slavery will seep into your pores and you will learn with conviction that where you fit into this taxonomy is far worse than the sharp edges of poor people on a sunny island. Now you'll fight for your life, except you'll never know if you're winning until you're too shattered to know the difference, or you're dead. All the while, people will look on saying that you've made something sturdy of your life, like a prison, so you'll remain in the hopes of living into their dreams for you—indentured. When you do return to that sunny island, the people won't feel quite so grating anymore, if only because they regard you as human, and you would have gone years without gulping a clean breath into fully human lungs. So from time to time on your trip you'll find yourself trying to breathe in your own humanity—but it won't work because now you're trained to take short, hollow breaths—you'll pant like a chimpanzee. You'll figure that without the ruthless training you may not have returned at all, so you'll develop a type of love for chastening. Maybe love is chastening. Perhaps being loved is being brutalized just enough to stay alive. You are alive… right?

But with this definition of love, you'll rather to be needed, not so much because you feel unworthy of love, but because there isn't enough left of you to withstand its cruelty. And this will be your coming to America—there will be nothing left of you as you are now to tell the story.

Myth Forlorn

Why are we enamored by the Phoenix? Before emerging anew from its own ash, it dies over and over again. The first Phoenix I'd ever encountered was Nanny of the Maroons, Jamaica's only female national hero. There are seven of them, six men and one woman who have received the country's highest order of distinction for their willingness to challenge colonialism and change the course of history for the Jamaican people. As a little girl, as soon as I'd laid eyes on her I wanted to be like Granny Nanny. Queen Nanny became our hero for her ferocious guerilla warfare against the British, and her success in freeing and protecting former slaves. Sometime around the 1750s, she met the untimely death that typically awaits courageous warriors who are out of step with their era. One day, I wasn't able to celebrate the mystery of Nanny's rebellion in the same ways anymore—I'd become uncomfortable learning that she was a spiritualist, engaging dark magic to beguile the British in her militarism. It wasn't a judgment so much as an acknowledgement that she was desperate to be free, and I couldn't glorify the wretchedness of grasping at liberation, like gulping for your last breath. Her death was combustion, not regeneration—there is nothing poetic in it. I wish they would all stop celebrating our survival when Nanny is still dead, and we are still not free.

Drown

There was something about all the scraping and tapping on my teeth I hated every time I went to the dentist, but I never did mind the suction. Once they got to work, cascades of saliva would flood the floor of my mouth, and with nowhere for it to go, I teetered on the edge of drowning in a pool of my body's own making. Luckily, the suction was on my side—it was always my salvation. All my life my mother had been my dentist. Incidentally, as a girl, she herself nearly drowned, but not of her own saliva. She never talked about it, but when she did she would always recount how surreal it was to be surrounded by cousins, aunts, and uncles while dying, with no one realizing she was letting go. Consequently, I went to grueling swim lessons every summer for weeks on end, even though I refused to put my face into the water—something about submersion unsettled me. I'd sit at the edge of the pool practicing to kick my legs while I baked under the oppressive afternoon sun for hours every day. Even though I only looked on from the margins, I willed myself faithfully to learn not to drown, concentrating steadily on the form and grace of my friends, who by now were swimming back and forth like fish. Sometimes my focus was so intense I could hear the subtle thumping of my head in my ears, and see the heat waves travelling across the cement to my stinging thighs. The whole drowning debacle could have been easily solved with a suction, at least in my imagination it would have. Sometimes I imagined inventing a giant suction that could rescue me from the water's grip if the need arose, but I never quite mastered the physics of it.

My father was like a suction, though, or he reminded me of one anyway. I'd sit for hours at the dinner table begging myself to finish all my rice and peas, chicken, potato salad, corn, and vegetables—not unlike the way I sat by the pool—and the task was similarly formidable. Without fail I'd look up in shock when only after my second or third bite, he was finished altogether, and what's more, there was no evidence of what had been sitting on his plate. Even the gravy disappeared. My father always ate things whole. He always got to leave the table, his suctioning saved him from the hold.

Strangely, when he moved out of our house, I was suddenly able to suction, too. It was like my body knew I needed new metaphysical capacity and instantly I could mindlessly guzzle and pulverize all of the foods my fingers could touch. I gulped my food in three bites, sometimes two, and after I ate, I'd lift the plate to my mouth to lick away all the evidence that food had been on it—sometimes hours later I'd find gravy on my nose. I couldn't even taste food anymore really. I too was eating something whole though I wasn't sure what. Suctioning food didn't make me buoyant, but I trusted the practice to keep me from drowning.

Years into my thirties and once safely tucked away in layers of heft, I read an article about drowning. It said that when it's happening, people can't breathe long enough to yell for help, they also can't wave for help, and in 20 to 60 seconds the entire drowning body is submerged. So fast, suction-fast, fast and invisible in plain sight. Without knowing it, I had sucked up my own submersion and drowned into myself whole.

Allostatic Rot

When the body is operating as it should, at equilibrium, it is described to be in homeostasis. When stress is introduced, the body engages the process of allostasis, as it regulates its anticipated needs, and satisfies them in an effort to return to homeostatic balance. If the body cannot return, it accumulates an allostatic load, and over time if the body continues to carry it, it weathers, another medical term for the long-term deleterious effects of racial trauma on Black bodies. According to the Journal of the National Medical Association, my Black body is quite literally weathering away (Duru et al., 2012). This means that other people's hatred for me and the resulting difficulty it poses in my life are likely to give me cancer, a stroke, heart disease, Type 2 diabetes, or some other debilitating condition that kills me. Somehow countering this eventuality is entirely in my charge, and an addition to my load. If I don't find a way to purge the constant deluge of anti-Blackness that has always been characteristic of everyday life for me, that violence and grief will rot me until there is nothing left. If I am too far gone, or too tired to fix this, it will cost me my life.

Impetus

When Sandra liking a boy at sixteen and showing him her affection meant that she was nasty and not cute, I was aware I would do something even before I decided.

When taking on the job of church groundskeeper meant that Mr. Williams and the other four members of his family would live their entire lives in one sixteen-by-twenty-foot room with curtains for doors on the church grounds, I was aware I would do something even before I decided.

When I felt I had no right to sit on my math tutor's verandah—where I was mandated to be for my lessons—because of his agitation in responding to what he imagined his neighbors might think of him, I was aware I would do something even before I decided.

When I went to the supermarket with adult male family members, and silence was the only acknowledgement of the various men who shamelessly called out to me in my ten-year-old school uniform, I was aware I would do something even before I decided.

When, try as I might, I just couldn't quite rule out the rumor that our woodshop teacher was sleeping with the pretty girl two years ahead of me and the tall girl I knew through my brother, I was aware I would do something even before I decided.

When I started to meet with mentors based on what I thought was the merit of my own achievement, and instead of asking me about my five-year goals, they asked if I was married, I was aware I would do something even before I decided.

When I couldn't be indignant about inappropriate advances just yet because my paychecks went as soon as they came, I was aware I would do something even before I decided.

When years into their adulthood, my aunt still hasn't told me who fathered her children for fear of shame and I never asked because I knew it was better for them, I was aware I would do something even before I decided.

When I wrote my first book about psychic colonization, and the publisher revised the title to remove the words "Black," "Woman," and "Third World," I was aware I would do something even before I decided.

I am aware I will do something. I will do something. I will do... something.

These Bodies Tell the Truth

My body knew before I did that something was wrong. It detected my mind's acceptance that I would not be loved, and resisted my transition into looking for ways to be needed. It tried to get a hold of me when I rehearsed leaving my voice's natural lower register for a higher, more approachable femininity. It protested for my worth with inexplicable and intermittent abdominal pangs throughout my adolescence and beyond, along my journey to remake myself as less proximate to what I am. It contended with me when I stopped believing its forewarning; instead I thought myself strong when I fought my way into spaces that felt perilous before I could prove they were fraught, or knew why they were threatening—and even after I knew, I fought to stay. I always fought with my body. I wore my body down to its wiring, and with the cables exposed, my synapses started to short and fire without warning. I winced, and flinched, and cringed, and jumped at nothing in particular—soon I could not make sense of myself, and I could not translate my body's faltering to the world around me.

A new sort of shame started seeping into my bones. I was ashamed of betraying my body these many years as I tried to transfigure it, but more precisely I was ashamed that I could not hide my own decomposition. One day, I demanded something of my body and it stopped altogether. With all its nameless injury, it would no longer trudge onward—it folded in on itself and began waiting to be healed. My body had made its last stand, but if left to me I would have kept going. My ransom payment was a confession of the self-hatred that drove me and my body into the ground, and my redemption from that grave was a bitter forgiveness for that treachery. My body is late, but it is returning. On the best day of my life, my body went completely quiet. Before that, I did not know my body absent of its protestations—is this blissful blankness what other bodies feel every day? It is still rare, but my body is sometimes free. I know now that somewhere in me is a reservoir to keep going, and I am careful not to wander back into a dogged existence I have been trained to mis-see as well-being.

When bodies like mine give out, there can be no substitution for surrender. The most decorated American gymnast in U.S. history enslaved her body to a relentless excellence the world could not deny, and even so when the bill came due for the dissonance of being celebrated by the entity responsible for her sexual exploitation, her body shut down its capacity to tell up from down, and she quit her entire career mid-Olympics. The number-two ranked women's tennis player in the world, and four-time Grand Slam champion, tried to wear the names of slain Black bodies on her person as she outperformed all of her peers, until one day her body also stopped, and she withdrew from Wimbledon at the peak of her career. We are no match for our bodies when they come to retrieve us from the places in which we can't remain—no matter how good we are or what we've trained them to do. The Black woman body always tells the truth.

Claudette

At fifteen years old—exactly nine months before Rosa Parks would go on to do the very same thing—Claudette Colvin refused to give up her seat on a bus in Montgomery, Alabama. She was both first, and quickly forgotten. That day she sat in a seat of her choosing, and when the bus driver ordered her to get up, she refused and cited her constitutional rights. Two police officers swiftly handcuffed, arrested, and jailed her, leaving her schoolbooks strewn across the seat she was forbidden. Colvin recalls that it was Black History Month, so something had stirred in her to fight. The National Association for the Advancement of Colored People decided not to platform Colvin's iconic sacrifice because her skin was too dark to woo public empathy. After having gone to jail, Colvin found herself shunned from the community she was fighting for, and consequently pregnant without the necessary support. Even in the fight for Black people, there is no place for a Black woman who is too Black.

Rosalie Walker Kept Hugging My Mother

I don't remember much about the second grade, but I do recall my growing infuriation with Rosalie Walker. We were not friends. Her plaits were longer and fuller than mine, her skin lighter, and she had no tummy pouch weighing in front of her the way I did. On just about every metric, she superseded me, but the straw that broke the proverbial camel's back was that every day she would hug my mother. Leaving school happened in a very predictable sequence. Before our final class for the day began, we'd stand and chorally recite: "Good afternoon, Mrs. Faberson, may God bless you and have a happy day!" After she invited us to sit, the lesson would begin, and at its conclusion, we would stand again to declare in unison: "School is over for today, we have done our work, and done our play. Before we go, we'd like to say, thank you Heavenly

Father for another day." Following that prayer we would sit to wait for our guardians to retrieve us, and mine was always my mother. When my mother arrived, it was my responsibility to collect my schoolbag, lunch box, and water bottle, and then walk to her "in an orderly fashion" for my hug and kiss.

Every day, while I was gathering my lunchbox and water bottle, Rosalie would spring up from her seat, and fasten herself tightly to my mother's legs in one fell swoop. Rosalie was stealing my mother. All of us had rules about when we could sit and stand, but fair-skinned Rosalie did not. I did not mind all the privileges girls like Rosalie enjoyed that I could not, but this was different—every day I blessed Mrs. Faberson and she repaid me by allowing Rosalie to take my mother away from me. My mind would race for a solution only to arrive at the dismal conclusion that there was nothing I could do. I wasn't allowed to jog or skip or run to my mother, so I was always too late for her first kiss. Rosalie, on the other hand, leapt toward her, and no one batted an eye, not even Mrs. Faberson. We all knew the rules were not the same for her. And as I stood and waited in daily agony for Rosalie to finish telling my mother the story of her day, I began to ask myself: Did my mother want the other children to think Rosalie was her daughter? Would she have preferred it? Is that why over time her eyes searched first for Rosalie? It was around this period of my understanding that I accepted that everything could be taken from darker girls, with push out bellies, and short plaits—even our own mothers could wish we were someone else.

The Last Stand

Can I forgive myself for a lifetime of self-hatred?

Now that I know that I was taught to loathe what I am, can I acknowledge that I complied?

Can I turn against what I was to survive what the world was to me?

Can I agree that the ever-elusive standard that would have awarded me worth would have continued to recede as I approached it?

Can I stop flinching and jumping and gasping for air when I notice things I didn't expect, even if they aren't surprising at all?

Can I write the shame out of my body, or does the confession make it more incarnate? Can I live the day in which my body stops waiting to be healed from the atrocity it has witnessed?

Will I ever broaden in the places pain has narrowed me?

Will my mind go quiet again?

Will the mysterious reservoir I draw from ever deny me one last sip? How do I remain among them without trivializing myself if what I truly am has menacing aptitude?

If I am able to stand still in myself at the cellular level, will I stop the transmissibility of these ugly pathologies?

Even if only here, am I a human?

References

Cooper, C. (2011, December 25). Drawing Sister P's tongue. *The Gleaner.* https://jamaica-gleaner.com/gleaner/20111225/cleisure/cleisure3.html

Duru, O. K., Harawa, N. T., Kermah, D., & Norris, K. C. (2012). Allostatic load burden and racial disparities in mortality. *Journal of the National Medical Association, 104*(1–2), 89–95. doi:10.1016/s0027-9684(15)30120-6

Gladwell, M. (2019, September 1). Malcolm Gladwell: "I'm just trying to get people to take psychology seriously." *The Guardian.* www.theguardian.com/books/2019/sep/01/malcolm-gladwell-interview-talking-to-strangers-apolitical

Jamaica Observer. (2012, April 19). Portia among *Time Magazine*'s 100 most influential. Jamaicaobserver.com. www.jamaicaobserver.com/news/Portia-among-Time-magazine-s-100-most-influential_11285578&template=MobileArticle

Kipling, R. (1895). Brother square toes. poetryfoundation.org. www.poetryfoundation.org/poems/46473/if---

3 Subjective Transmigration

In this section, I explore the phenomenon of *subjective transmigration*. Anthropologists Nina Glick Schiller, Linda Basch, and Cristina Szanton Blanc (1995) describe a "transmigrant" as one who is rooted in both their new country and integrally engaged with their country of origin. Transmigrants have established a home in their in-betweenness. I take up the idea of transmigration to extend to the enigmatic subjective space of homemaking. In this engagement, I examine the psychic reality of the subaltern inhabitation of nowhere in particular. The collection of vignettes related to my theory of *subjective transmigration* precedes from a fulsome appraisal of suppositions about transmigrancy, which hold that "transmigrants are immigrants whose daily lives depend on multiple and constant interconnections across international borders and whose public identities are configured in their relationship to more than one nation-state" (Schiller et al., 1995, p. 48). In this section, I probe these identity configurations at the subjective locus, essentializing the solitary and bewildering experience of performing home while being scattered across geopolitical coordinates. In other words, I explore what it means to be lost, in a sense, wherever one is physically situated. Home then exists only within one's subjective personhood. In this section, there is deliberate attending to the intangible affliction of being locked into subjective transmigration, and the lived outcomes that metabolize from that stasis.

The themes explored within subjective transmigration include: the social capital of colonization, the internalized immutable inferiority of colonized beings, self-denigration, self-abandonment, self-contempt, shape-shifting for survival across real and imagined borders, the loss of original form, the decay and death of home as it was, the extinction of returning, the condemnation of ill-suitedness, self-impersonation, self-alterity, and absence.

DOI: 10.4324/9781003226802-4

Afro Saxon

During the reign of King Charles II, the tradition emerged of British barristers adorning themselves with horsehair lock wigs in addition to their heavy robes (Discover Britain, 2022). The custom came to England by way of France, as a means to remain presentable while cutting one's hair short enough to keep away parasites before the advent of hot running water. This hardly explains why nearly four centuries later, in the year 2020, the Speaker of the House of Representatives in a former colony in the Caribbean is still wearing one, and what's more, he is not alone.

The high courts of many former British colonies continue in the convention of the traditional barrister's wig in spite of the substantial expense required to procure one. Over time, members of the Caribbean intelligentsia have made attempts to deconstruct the pathology. One such effort by pyschohistoriographers Frederick Hickling and Gerard Hutchinson (1999) produced the concept of "breadfruit psychosis" which they describe as "precipitated by the recognition that the immutable inferiority lumbered on Black people by European racism is difficult to dislodge." Though not from the Caribbean himself, Critical Theorist Homi Bhabha reanimates the concept of "mimicry"—which Lacan (1978) explains as "one of the most elusive and effective strategies of colonial power and knowledge"—to examine formerly colonized peoples. In comparison, philosopher Lloyd Best (1965) proposed the idea of the "Afro Saxon," a Black man in the Caribbean who somehow thinks himself White. There are many ways to say we are not at home in ourselves, but rather, still searching for something otherwise. It is a type of madness that deceives us into rationalizing our own denigration and self-hatred. Yet the syndrome is invisible to its victims. They say we have a cultural schizophrenia, and what they say may well be right.

Papered Over

To move across national borders is, in a way, to transcend states of matter—to become human in a different place. To traverse worlds—the first world, the second world, the third world, or as we refer to it in the present day, the developing worlds and the developed ones—is to transmogrify out of humanity into something more performative, something that never leaves the lamina beneath the skin. That crust etches away a more honest knowledge of who we are, in favor of a romanticizing of what we left, leaving us in constant disillusionment about where we are going. Where do sub-humans go and how do they get there? At first, we learn to shape-shift as an act of survival, but soon enough, we can never return to our original form. Before we know better, we think of our-selves as elastic bands, always bouncing back to be exactly as we were, but eventually we find we are more like paper—malleable of course, but once we are crushed and flattened out again, all the creases show. Those lines make us older, more distorted, harder to recognize when we go home. But where is home for crushed paper masquerading mint condition? It won't go where it used to, and even when it hides in a stack, all of its deformities set it apart. It cannot hide. No two pieces of paper are crushed just alike, so it can't even make home with others who have made the subdermal voyage. Just as we never truly return to ourselves, home will not wait for us. We must make home inward and alone, settling into its extinction.

Grounding

We think of the heart biologically because it is in our bodies, but it functions more accurately like an electrical system. Each of the respective chambers alternatively contracts and relaxes, pumping blood into the rest of our members. Every spasm is triggered by electrical pulses that travel down a node at the center of the organ, and the process is so seamless that with just a finger to the wrist, you can feel your body pul-sate in unison with each beat.

The earth's core is similar to the heart in that way—we think of it geo-logically because of its situating, but it also functions electrically. The interior of the earth sends out heat that naturally converts itself into con-vection currents of molten iron and nickel, and the movement of these currents then becomes electric. Both the body and the earth emit elec-tromagnetic fields. The birds obey the earth's magnetosphere, using it as a compass to navigate their migrations, but for us it is not as simple. Even when the earth taps into our wiring and pulls us in toward the place we're intended to be, sometimes we still walk away. We fight that pull and are torn asunder, condemned to suffer an ill-suitedness of not knowing how to be where we are at the molecular level, particularly since all of our being can't be there. Geobiologist Isaac Hilburn conducted a study that found a connection between human magnetoreceptivity and the alpha-band oscillations in our brains that indicate we are at rest (Wilke, 2019). We are repelled in the earth while we try to make home in between the poles. The pulses won't syncopate, and the heart and mind can't find intermission. We become refractory, disordered, making homes that can't completely live up to the name. There can be no true homemaking in-between, but we still try. Perhaps this is why those bodies were falling from the sky in Kabul as they tried to make migrations against the pull of the earth. What if the earth pulls you into a place where you won't survive? When the poles of the heart and the earth are in disagreement, even that repulsion can kill a man several times over—it can kill a man every day.

No Longer King

Post-emancipation, some Jamaican people began allowing their hair to grow into locs as a retaliatory statement against Eurocentric norms that were imposed on their bodies under British rule. Even without an explicitly Euro-dominant governance in place, Jamaican society remained principally Eurocentric. For example, most people referred to the hairstyle as "dreadful," and in this way the term "dreadlocks" developed etymologically. Dreadlocks in Jamaica are now most readily associated with the Rastafarian religion, which requires its participants to take the Nazarite Vow, based on an Old Testament edict in the Holy Bible: "Leviticus 21:5 'They shall not make baldness upon their head, neither shall they shave off the corner of their beard nor make any cuttings in their flesh'" (Grant, 2020).

Nzinga King took this vow, but she would not keep it. Though her consecrated crown was sanctified by a venerable Bishop within the Nyabingi order, her locs would fall away on July 22, 2021. Nzinga took a taxi-cab that day, and while she was in it, the driver was pulled over for transporting unmasked passengers during a pandemic. Though Nzinga, a nursing student, was not one of them, she would still be subject to the police spraying mace into the car at all of its passengers. When Nzinga fled the vehicle, she shrieked at the officers and was detained for disorderly conduct. While in custody for six days, she would suffer the indignity of a strip search that required the removal of her underwear, a six-day stay on a concrete floor, and the sentence of enduring her menstrual cycle without the aid of any sanitary amenities. What's more is Nzinga was taken into custody with her sacred locs, but released back into society without them. She told the media a policewoman cut them off at the station, and later three anonymous sources claimed she cut them herself. At only 19 years old, Nzinga recalls that the cutting of her locs reminds her of when she was raped by a gang only three years prior—for her it felt the same. In the end, Nzinga King has no crown.

Fugue

I didn't know Janay well, but our beds were nearby each other's at camp. They told us that because of Jesus, her mother would not die. But she did. Three months later, Janay's father remarried her mother's best friend. The congregation deemed it disgraceful, and even though many left, most couldn't look away from the spectacle. Things seemed to be finally calm again six months later when Pastor Kalter fell into a permanent vegetative state. He had publicly refused his medication, assuring all onlookers that because of Jesus he was healed. He remained dormant and unresponsive for decades, until he died quietly one day, without an audience.

I couldn't name the precise event that launched me out of my body into a dissociative fugue, but somewhere between 13 and 14 years old, it feels like I left altogether. I wandered outside of my body, trying on new identities until I was 26, and found final rest in a Christ-centered heuristic, while simultaneously deeply situated in study about the brutal, savage violence of colonization as effected through the Christian church. I thought often of Pastor Kalter, but did not know what to do with his memory. I expected one day that the threads holding me together at the seams of that fissure—at the intersection of my memories of those broken Jesus promises, my Blackness, and my commitment to this Christ—would tear me apart, but instead, the errors in my theology were deconstructed and put back together in ways that wrote me into it.

I came home to myself in the White evangelical church. Without the comfort of psychogenic fugue, my memory was no longer disrupted, and seeded into my consciousness was an uneasy awareness of the impossible distance between that Christ and this church. This White supremacist church. This Black sensationalist church. This misogynoiristic church. This violently silent church. This performatively deceptive church. This dance over dead Black bodies to celebrate other things that really mattered church. This hurt me to control me church. This never keeps its promises church. This White Jesus, White Savior, White Domination church. This American nationalist church. This incomplete understanding church. This Black people are the problem church. This won't face its own history and complicity church. This manipulate you to get what I need while your life passes by you church.

The word "fugue" comes from the Latin word for "flight." I won't fly away from this church. I won't let you have this church. I will not cede my country to White supremacy or colonialism, and neither will I cede my church. I am not confused about this church. This church is the place where I came home. This church is the place that He calls home. This church is the place that I call home. This church will always keep a place for me.

Migrational Memory

My hair, wherever it goes, will take with it the charring memory of being made to do what it will never naturally do, week after week, year after year, until it fell out altogether.

My forehead, wherever it goes, will take with it the phantom kiss that never came at night, when the feeling of being tucked in converted itself into being locked away when things got darker in our house.

My eyebrows, wherever they go, will take with them the welts and bruises of being waxed away and ripped asunder to look less like brooms and more like shapes I've never seen as endemic to any face.

My eyes, wherever they go, will take with them the image of my friends' fathers and our male teachers ogling us before we understood who we were—before we knew that what we were was broader than their desire.

My nose, wherever it goes, will take with it the smell of urine mixed with bleach that engulfed me on every single one of my weekly visits to the children's home to sit with girls who knew as well as I did that they were living out a tragedy of heroic proportion. I was only there on punishment, my nose never acclimated—I could smell it every minute we sat drenched in its intensity.

My lips, wherever they go, will take with them the sting of a sharply bristling mustache making small cuts all around my teenage mouth. I did want the kiss, but sometimes the outline of my upper lip still feels rubbed raw.

My ears, wherever they go, will take with them the sound of loud white men shouting in my island from the base of their hefty guts, laughing so forcefully it hurt my ears—it hurts my chest still. I never have to summon the memory of them laughing at what they do to us, as it's always in my head.

My neck, wherever it goes, will take with it the muscular recollection of how appalled they were when it refused to bow, when it stood turgid so I wouldn't avert my gaze, when my neck wouldn't apologize for wrongs no one else was punished for, when it wouldn't betray me by displaying the shame I felt in my melting center.

My shoulders, wherever they go, will take with them the souvenir of your rough, oversized, unwelcome hands gripping them during our meeting. These shoulders sent bullets into my spine, got me out of my chair, and chastised me not to need your help or go back into your office.

These are only the corporeal memories that I want to share—others still travel with me. Believe me, all of me remembers.

Monkeys and Coconuts

In 1868, W.E.B. Du Bois was born in Great Barrington, Massachusetts to a relatively well-off family in a moderately tolerant and integrated neighborhood. Du Bois would go on to become the first African American to earn his doctorate at Harvard University, and found the National Association for the Advancement of Colored People (NAACP). In 1887, The Right Excellent Marcus Mosiah Garvey was born in St. Ann's Bay, St. Ann in Jamaica to a stonemason and a household servant. One of 11 siblings, Marcus would found the Universal Negro Improvement Association and African Communities League (UNIA-ACL) and the Black Star Line shipping and passenger company.

Both men were extraordinarily influential voices working toward Black liberation and advancement within the same era. I wondered why then, with such a critical mandate in common, I was so unsurprised to read Du Bois' critique of his contemporary, Marcus Garvey: "Many American Negroes viewed Garvey's meteoric rise as the enthroning of a dema-gogue, who with monkey shines was deluding the people and taking their hard-earned dollars" (The Marcus Garvey and UNIA Papers Project, 2021, emphasis added). Monkey shines.

With a similar instinct, in August 2021, American track sensation Sha'Carri Richardson finished sixth at the highly anticipated 100m dash at the Prefontaine Classic, the final qualifying event for the Tokyo 2020 Olympics. Runners from Jamaica placed first, second, and third in the race, with the winner earning the second-fastest time in the competition's history, and a Diamond League record. Following the race, Richardson officially endorsed a comment on one of her social media platforms that also left me unsurprised: "Not y'all Jamaicans still talking sh*t when y'all gotta walk barefoot to your coconut stand everyday for a living" (TMZ Sports, 2021). Coconut stand.

It is this uneasy attachment that keeps me unsure of the kinship between us. Are we—African Americans and Afro Caribbeans—truly indivisible? We are inter-connected to be sure, but something in our relating has fallen short of true integration. When it suits, we are disposable, and worse, through the cracks we see that we are somehow far less human to you than we thought. More monkey than man—perhaps apes.

Dis-appearing Black

I had a naïve expectation that I believe all immigrants share: that my Blackness would proliferate in the convening of my destination. I had hoped to change the soil, to make it richer in some way. I had hoped to dash my spices, pronunciations, choreographies, memories, and wisdoms like seed into new ground, but there was no place for them here. When I touched that alien dirt, I was translated—sterilized of everything I hoped to bring. Those nostalgic artifacts drifted out of my hands and pockets long before I knew they were gone. I had no hope of recovery—I do not know when they were taken away. I am not sure if they were seized or given, I have only a faint remembrance of feeling like an impersonation of what I used to be one day, and I hated myself for it. I forfeited the residue—it wasn't enough to make me whole. I was erased, reshaped, rebuilt, and ill of insincere affirmation. I witnessed the persecution of their Blackness on their own soil, and I wept for them. When they turned on me, I had no tears left. I had no self left. Without my artifacts, I had no home left. This is the double witnessing of transnational Blackness—it is always absorbed into an invisible wake (Sharpe, 2016).

In 1974, Antiguan immigrant Louchland Henry penned these words about what was left of him:

New York is anonymous
Among millions as he strolls

New York City is a story
That will never be told

And despite it all, New York is my home.
I feel fiercely loyal to this acquired homeland.
Because of New York I am foreigner in whatever other place…

But New York City is not the city of my infancy…
Because of that I will always remain on the margin, a stranger
   between
these rocks…

Then, now and forever, I will always remain a foreigner
Even when I return to the city of my infancy.

I will always carry this marginality…
too habanera to be a New Yorker
too New Yorker to be
… ever to become again…
anything else.

(Bryce-Laporte, 1989)

Revision

While living in the United States, from birth to six years old, I remember myself as very present and clear in mind. My parents described me as talkative, precocious, and full of laughter. I remember constant discovery, and a nearly unending parade of happy events, and loving people. I was a girl who was dearly loved in Beltsville, Maryland. When we moved to Jamaica, though, the smells were strange, and everything seemed to be cracked, or crumbling in some way. There was a general unfinishedness about all of it, but its scenic charm was undeniable; somehow the blemishes made it more beautiful than perfection could. Jamaica was a mystical place that way. I did not smile or laugh as much there, and I was not nearly as brave. I became watchful, so much so that I could see the people I observed recoiling at my glaring eeriness. I thought longer about what to say, I did not know what I was expected to say—but I had hard learned that if I said what I wanted without thought, conversations would fall suddenly silent, and shift abruptly away from centering my engagement. I was misunderstood there, a naughty girl who yelled, lost her temper, and was constantly disappointing. I was always sad. They didn't mind my sadness, so I made them reckon with my disrespect.

When it was time for me to return to the United States at 18, I decided I would be light and jovial there. I wanted to recover the version of myself that was dearly loved in Beltsville. I imagined myself immersed in scores of friends, laughing loudly, sharing thoughtlessly about whatever was in my head. Instead, I arrived an object of male desire and White curiosity—a caricature with no dimension. I became even more remote from who I always thought I would one day be. I fought to keep from crying, and did damage I could not repair. I blamed the backwardness in the air in Richmond, Virginia for who I was there, and set my sights next on Washington, D.C. The nation's capital enthralled me—I knew I'd finally found my home. Here, I was smart, witty, sometimes badly behaved, but earnestly learning—earnestly growing. I moved in and out of diaspora communities to cultivate a collective remembrance of the astonishingly alluring gentle decay of home. The home of childhood that never fully understood me, but in the end learned to accept me as its own. Now when I visit home, I sense my regression into making split-second decisions that even I don't understand—desperate to be understood. When my jokes fall flat or hang in the air between us, I grow angry, cold. I am always just one single hair away from rage. I feel the pull of each place's interpretation of me, luring me into being, shaped by its empathetic rendering of what it understands me to be. But I cannot be what I was for you to join me here in what I am, so we are in two different places, even when we are not apart. We are in two places—I am in three, sometimes four—and in a breath, I am always returning.

Stuck Nowhere

Following a traumatic event, the brain attempts to process why the wound happened and what it means about the self. Typically, the defective rationale that emerges in response to these questions keeps the self from moving on from the ordeal. Those justifications, or cognitive distortions, are called "stuck points" because the thoughts keep you stuck in place, essentially unable to recover. In a way then, worse than the trauma itself is the way the brain changes after to keep you reliving it.

I am stuck in many places. I am still in Spain with the many men on the streets who kept asking me how much I cost on my walk home from school. Am I a prostitute? I am still standing outside of the library in South Africa with the sun pelting on my soot black neck, hearing I can't come inside in a predominantly colored area. Am I dirty? I am still on the bus in Virginia with that White girl from my class who told me I passed because my teacher was political. Am I inferior? I am still in Jamaica feeling the hot breath and spray from that angry white man hitting my face like heat waves. Am I worthless? I am still at my front door in Maryland watching that service provider take one look at me and walk away without speaking. Am I disgusting? I am still hearing my Hispanic teacher tell me if I take the test, I'll probably pass it but only barely. Am I hopeless? I am still reading the office newsletter in Washington, D.C. with pictures from everyone's gardens and accounts about the weekend, but no mention of the state-sanctioned murder of a black body that fell silently on the street days before. Am I here? Am I here? Am I here?

References

Best, L. (1965). From Chaguaramas to slavery. *New World Quarterly*, *2*, 10.

Bryce-Laporte, R. S. (1989). New York City and the new Caribbean immigration: A contextual statement. *International Migration Review*, *13*(2), 214–234, https://doi.org/10.2307/2545029

Discover Britain. (2020). British law: The tradition of wigs. *Discover Britain Mag*. www.discoverbritainmag.com/british-law-wigs/

Glick Schiller, N., Basch, L., & Szanton Blanc, C. (1995). From immigrant to transmigrant: Theorizing transnational migration. *Anthropological Quarterly*, 68(1), 48–63. https://doi.org/10.2307/3317464

Grant, C. A. (2020, August 3). Learn the origins of the dreadlocks hairstyle & Rastafarianism in Jamaica. *scholarshipJamaica.com*. https://scholarshipjamaica.com/rastafarianism-dreadlocks-hairstyle/

Hickling, F., & Hutchinson, G. (1999). Roast breadfruit psychosis: Disturbed racial identification in African-Caribbeans. *Psychiatric Bulletin, 23*(3), 132–134. doi:10.1192/pb.23.3.132

Lacan, J. (1978). The line and light. In *The four fundamental concepts of psychoanalysis* (trans. A. Sheridan; pp. 91–104). Norton.

Sharpe, C. (2016). *In the wake: On Blackness and being.* Duke University Press.

The Marcus Garvey and UNIA Papers Project. (2021). *American Series introduction, Volume 1: 1826–August 1919.* UCLA African Studies Center. www.international.ucla.edu/asc/mgpp/intro01

TMZ Sports. (2021, August 25). Sha'Carri Richardson: Runner's Twitter "likes" offensive. *TMZ.* www.tmz.com/2021/08/25/shacarri-richardson-twitter-likes-offensive-tweet-about-jamaicans/

Wilke, C. (2019, March 19). Can humans sense magnetic fields? *The Scientist.* www.the-scientist.com/news-opinion/can-humans-sense-the-magnetic-field--65611

Epilogue

This book's novel exploration of the confines, inscriptions, and slippages of identity formation for the postcolonial Anglo-Caribbean Black subaltern has demonstrated a willingness to put contemporary political discourse in conversation with heavier humanities theory to propose new possibilities for Black subaltern humanity. I revisit the two quintessential questions around which this exploration was designed: *Is the Black subaltern really there?* And if truly present, *Can the Black subaltern be fully human?* I approach these pivotal questions by attending to the thematic realities related to discontinuity, reconfiguration, destabilization, and deliberate transgression in the sojourn of humanizing the subaltern through the immutable sentiments of Jamaican revolutionary Mutabaruka, whose name translates to "the one is who is always victorious":

> *Dis poem*
> *Shall speak of the wretched sea*
> *that washed ships to these shores*
> *of mothers crying for their young*
> *swallowed up by the sea*
>
> *Dis poem shall say nothing new;*
> *Dis poem shall speak of time,*
> *Time unlimited; time undefined*
> *Dis poem shall call names*
> *Names like: Lumumba, Kenyatta, Nkrumah*
> *Hannibal, Akhenaten, Malcolm, Garvey*
> *Haile Selassie*

DOI: 10.4324/9781003226802-5

Dis poem is vexed about apartheid, racism, fascism
the Klu Klux klan, riots in Brixton, Atlanta,
Jim Jones

Dis poem is revolting against First World, Second World,
Third World
Division; man-made decision

Dis poem is like all the rest
Dis poem will not be amongst great literary works,
Will not be recited by poetry enthusiasts
It will not be quoted by politicians, nor men of religion

Dis poem is knives, guns, bombs
Blazing for freedom
Yes! dis poem is a drum
Ashanti, Mau Mau, Ibo, Yoruba, Nyabinghi Warriors
Uhuru Uhuru
Uhuru Namibia
Uhuru Soweto
Uhuru Afrika

Dis poem will not change things
Dis poem needs to be changed
Dis poem is a rebirth of a people
Arising, awakening, understanding

Dis poem speak
Is speaking
Has spoken
Dis poem shall continue even when poets have stopped writing
Dis poem shall survive you, me… it shall linger in history
In your mind
In time; forever

Dis poem is time; only time will tell
Dis poem is still not written
Dis poem has no poet
Dis poem is just a part of the story
His-story, her-story, our-story, the story still untold

Dis poem is now ringing, talking, irritating
Making you want to stop it
But dis poem will not stop

Dis poem is long; cannot be short
Dis poem cannot be tamed, cannot be blamed
The story is still not told about dis poem

Dis poem is old; new
Dis poem was copied from the Bible, your prayer book
Playboy magazine, the New York Times, Readers Digest
the CIA files, the KGB files
Dis poem is no secret

Dis poem shall be called: boring, stupid, senseless
Dis poem is watching you try to make sense of dis poem
Dis poem is messing up your brain
Making you want to stop listening to dis poem
But you shall not stop listening to dis poem
You need to know what will be said next in dis poem
Dis poem shall disappoint you
Because
Dis poem is to be continued in your mind, in your mind,
in your mind, in your mind

In the year 2021, while still in the grip of a global pandemic, Haiti and its people endured floods, hunger, violence, a coup d'état, hurricane devastation, earthquakes, and the wholesale pullout of its aid-based infrastructure. It is very nearly a failed state. Many of its residents have in turn sought humanitarian support and asylum within the borders of the United States of America. Of course, humanitarianism is categorically reserved for human beings, and as such, the question persists: Are we human? We were not yet human in 2021.

Can the Black Subaltern Be Human?

In 2016, Black Studies mastermind Christina Sharpe wrote *In the Wake: On Blackness and Being*, and in the text, she "activat[es] multiple registers of 'wake'—the path behind a ship…coming to consciousness … illustrat[ing] how Black lives are swept up and animated by the afterlives of slavery." Sharpe "delineates what survives despite such insistent violence and negation … show[ing] how the sign of the slave ship marks and haunts contemporary Black life in the diaspora and how the specter of the hold produces conditions of containment, regulation, and punishment, but also something in excess of them." In the weather, "Sharpe situates anti-Blackness and white supremacy as the total climate that produces premature Black death as normative" (Duke University Press, 2016).

Something in Excess of Them

Amidst a barrage of profane imagery from the year 2021—featuring broken Haitian bodies wading through murky frontier waters into New Worlds, while white men on horseback whip and trample them—I grow even more doubtful that the Black subaltern will ever be free. The sheer horror of what they have done to us, the sport of it, the world's indulgence.

> When I search for Man in the technique and the style of Europe, I see only a succession of negations of man, and an avalanche of murders. The human condition, plans for mankind and collaboration between men in those tasks which increase the sum total of humanity are new problems, which demand true inventions. Let us decide not to imitate Europe; let us combine our muscles and our brains in a new direction. Let us try to create the whole man, whom Europe has been incapable of bringing to triumphant birth.
>
> (Fanon, 1965)

References

Duke University Press. (2016). *In the wake: On Blackness and being*, by Christina Sharpe. www.dukeupress.edu/in-the-wake

Fanon, F. (1965). *The wretched of the earth*. www.marxists.org/subject/africa/fanon/conclusion.htm

Mutabaruka. (1995). "Dis poem." *Review: Literature and Arts of the Americas*, *28*(50), 52–53. https://doi.org/10.1080/08905769508594431

Patterson, O. (2018). *Slavery and social death: A comparative study, with a new preface*. Harvard University Press.

Index